D0965786

NATURAL LANGUAGE PROCESSING IN THE 1980s

CSLI
Lecture Notes
Number 12

NATURAL LANGUAGE PROCESSING IN THE 1980s

A BIBLIOGRAPHY

Gerald Gazdar, Alex Franz,
Karen Osborne, and Roger Evans

CENTER FOR THE STUDY
OF LANGUAGE
AND INFORMATION

Randall Library UNC-W

CSLI was founded early in 1983 by researchers from Stanford University, SRI International, and Xerox PARC to further research and development of integrated theories of language, information, and computation. CSLI headquarters and the publication offices are located at the Stanford site.

CSLI/SRI International   **CSLI/Stanford**   **CSLI/Xerox PARC**
333 Ravenswood Avenue   Ventura Hall   3333 Coyote Hill Road
Menlo Park, CA 94025   Stanford, CA 94305 Palo Alto, CA 94304

Copyright ©1987
Center for the Study of Language and Information
Leland Stanford Junior University

Library of Congress Cataloging-in-Publication Data

Natural language processing in the 1980s.

(CSLI lecture notes ; no. 13)
Includes indexes.
1. Linguistics—Data processing—Bibliography.
I. Gazdar, Gerald. II. Series.
Z7004.L3N37   1987   [P98]   016.41'028'5   87–27644
ISBN 0–937073–28–8 (Paper)
ISBN 0–937073–26–1 (Cloth)

Library of Congress Catalog Card Number: 87–71618

Printed in the United States

P
98
.N37
1987

Introduction

THE AIM of this book is to make available, in a readily accessible form, bibliographic information about the vast majority of 1980s publications in the field of natural language processing (NLP) and computational linguistics. To this end, it contains 1764 numbered references to papers and books in the field published (or republished) since January 1980. These references are ordered alphabetically by first author, so if you know the identity of the first author of the item that you are trying to chase down, then you can look it up directly. There is, in addition, an index of subsidiary authors that lists, for each such author, the numbers of the papers on which that author appears as a second or subsequent author.

If your concern is to access papers by topic, rather than by author, then this book provides an extensive keyword-in-context (KWIC) index based on the titles of all the papers. Users of KWIC indexes should, however, bear in mind their limitations. If you simply wish to recover details of a paper based on your recollection of words in the title, then it is likely to be helpful. But if you wish to find all the papers on ATNs, then looking up "ATN" will only get you part of the way: not every paper dealing with ATNs uses the acronym in the title (though many do), some use "augmented transition network" instead, whilst others contain nothing in their title that unambiguously signals the nature of their content. Finally, it should be noted that some words, "natural," "language," "comput...," for example, show up in titles so frequently that their inclusion in the KWIC index would have doubled the length (and the cost) of this book, so they have been excluded.

No bibliography of an active and diverse interdisciplinary research area can lay claim to full comprehensiveness. Our aim has been to exhaustively cover the core sources in the field and to augment the result with as many items from other sources as we could readily lay our hands on. We have excluded from our remit unpublished papers, dissertations, and technical reports containing only papers by authors based at the issuing institution. The core of the bibliography consists of all the papers in the journal *Computational Linguistics*, all the books and papers in

v

books published in the ACL (Association for Computational Linguistics) book series "Studies in Natural Language Processing," all the papers republished in *Readings in Natural Language Processing* (1986, edited by Grosz, Sparck Jones, and Webber), all the papers to be found in the conference proceedings volumes of ACL, European ACL, COLING, TINLAP (Theoretical Issues in Natural Language Processing) and TANLU (Theoretical Aspects of Natural Language Understanding), together with all the papers on natural language processing to be found in the journals *Artificial Intelligence* and *Computational Intelligence,* and in the conference proceedings volumes of AAAI (American Association for Artificial Intelligence), AISB (Society for the Study of Artificial Intelligence and the Simulation of Behaviour), ECAI (European Conference on Artificial Intelligence), and IJCAI (International Joint Conference on Artificial Intelligence).[1]

This core has been augmented by individual papers drawn from numerous journals, conference and workshop proceedings, ad hoc publications, the contents of most of the edited collections on NLP, and by the rather few texts and monographs that we know to have been published on the topic. In selecting non-core items for inclusion, we have excluded papers published in languages other than English (though there are a few non-English papers from our core sources that are included for the sake of complete coverage of those sources) and we have used the question "would the editor of *Computational Linguistics* consider this paper a relevant submission to the journal?" as a very rough guide for deciding whether or not to include details of a paper. No doubt certain anomalous items have crept in, however. Although historically subsumed under the rubric "computational linguistics," papers on such topics as concordance creation, lexicostatistics, author identification, and the like have not been necessarily included, though, where such papers showed up in sources we have covered, then their details are included. By contrast, we have made some effort to ensure that NLP work in the logic programming tradition was well represented, even though much of this appears in the logic programming literature rather than in our core sources.

This bibliography was put together using the Berkeley Unix 'refer' system on a Sun 3/160 at the University of Sussex. One of the less significant advantages of compiling a big bibliography under such a system (as opposed to using file cards, say) is the ease with which certain statistics can be extracted. Since these figures may help the user get a sense of the object in hand, we will list some of them here. Of the 1764 listed items, about 50 are duplicates, partly a reflection of the fact that certain authors in

---

[1] This August 1987 edition of the bibliography contains items from the first two 1987 issues of *Computational Linguistics,* the 1987 AAAI, IJCAI, and ACL proceedings, but not those from the as yet unavailable proceedings of the 1987 European ACL meeting.

this field have taken to publishing the same paper in two different conference proceedings volumes. The papers distribute over years of publication roughly as follows:

1980:	210
1981:	140
1982:	210
1983:	240
1984:	220
1985:	250
1986:	350
1987:	160

These papers involve a total of around 1350 distinct individuals as authors or coauthors, although this figure does not reveal how common multiple authorship is in this area (papers average 1.6 authors each). The most prolific author represented, by quite a large margin, is Aravind Joshi, other researchers with a dozen or more papers listed are Douglas Appelt, Robert Berwick, Jaime Carbonell, Eugene Charniak, Philip Cohen, Barbara Grosz, Philip Hayes, Jerry Hobbs, Martin Kay, Wendy Lehnert, Fernando Pereira, David McDonald, Kathleen McKeown, Graeme Ritchie, Stuart Shieber, Karen Sparck-Jones, Bonnie Lynn Webber, Ralph Weischedel, and Yorick Wilks. Since more than a third of this group of people have had long-standing CSLI affiliations, the appearance of this bibliography in the CSLI house series is perhaps appropriate.

The bibliography source files are now kept on-line at Stanford University and can be accessed by computer mail by people with access to the relevant academic network. Send computer mail to

clbib@russell.stanford.edu

with the single word "help" in the "Subject:" field in order to receive instructions on searching the bibliography automatically by mail.

Machine readable copies of the current main 'refer' source file can be obtained on a single 360K DS/DD MS-DOS format floppy disk (the *only* available format) for $16, payable with order, from Ms. Sheila Lee (CLBIB), School of Cognitive Sciences, University of Sussex, Brighton BN1 9QN, UK.

This bibliography is an ongoing enterprise—the computer version will be kept up to date, and it is anticipated that there will be subsequent editions of this book. Users of the book who notice clear lacunae or errors are urged to write with full details to CLBIB (Gazdar/Evans), School of Cognitive Sciences, University of Sussex, Brighton BN1 9QN, UK. Likewise, book publishers and conference organizers are invited to send relevant new publications to that address if they wish to ensure prompt coverage of the material therein.

We are grateful to Jennifer Ballentine (Morgan Kaufmann), Jim Hunter (Sussex), Dikran Karagueuzian (Stanford), Sheila Lee (Sussex), Alison Mudd (Sussex), Brigitte Ohlig (UCSC), Emma Pease (Stanford) William

Poser (Stanford), Roger Sinnhuber (Sussex), Aaron Sloman (Sussex), Don Walker, Mary McGee Wood (UMIST), and the InterLibrary Loans Office of the Sussex University Library for their help with various aspects of this enterprise, to Jeff Goldberg (Stanford) for the major Unix/refer/Tib/TEX expertise that made the printed version possible, to Alvey/SERC (UK) for grant support to Evans, and to the ESRC (UK) and SERC (UK) for grant support to Gazdar.

—The Editors

Computational Linguistics in the 1980s

1. Aarts, Jan and Theo van den Heuvel. 1985. Computational tools for the syntactic analysis of corpora. *Linguistics* 23:2, 303–335.

2. Abe, Masahiro, Yoshimitsu Ooshima, Katsuhiko Yuura and Nobo-yuki Takeichi. 1986. A Kana-Kanji translation system for non-segmented input sentences based on syntactic and semantic analysis. In *COLING-86*, 280–285.

3. Abe, Norihiro, Nobutaka Uemura, Masahiro Higashide and Saburo Tsuji. 1980. On FROFF: a text processing system for English texts and figures. In *COLING-80*, 262–269.

4. Abe, Norihiro, Itsuya Soga and Saburo Tsuji. 1981. A plot under-standing system on reference to both image and language. *IJCAI-81* 1, 77–84.

5. Abe, Norihiro and Saburo Tsuji. 1982. A learning of object struc-tures by verbalism. In *COLING-82*, 1–6.

6. Abe, Norihiro, Fumihide Itoh and Saburo Tsuji. 1982. Towards a learning of object models using analogical objects and verbal instruction. In *AAAI-82*, 362–366.

7. Abramson, Harvey. 1984. Definite clause translation grammars. In *1984 International Symposium on Logic Programming*. IEEE Computer Society Press, Silver Spring, MD, 233–240.

8. Abramson, Harvey. 1985. Definite clause translation grammars and the logical specification of data types as unambiguous con-text free grammars. In *Proceedings of an International Workshop on Natural Language Understanding and Logic Programming, Uni-versity of Rennes*.

1

9. Abramson, Harvey, Veronica Dahl, Lynette Hirschman and Paul Sabatier. 1985. Logic Metagrammars - some controversial issues. In *Theoretical Approaches to Natural Language Understanding, a Workshop at Halifax, Nova Scotia*, 10.

10. Abramson, Harvey. 1986. Sequential and concurrent deterministic logic grammars. In *Proceedings of the Third International Conference on Logic Programming*, Ehud Shapiro, (ed.) Springer, Berlin, 389–395.

11. Adam, Anne and Jean-Pierre Laurent. 1980. Automatic diagnostics of semantic errors. In *AISB-80*, 1–10.

12. Adorni, Giovanni, A. Boccalatte and Mauri Di Manzo. 1982. Cognitive models for computer vision. In *COLING-82*, 7–12.

13. Adorni, Giovanni, Mauri Di Manzo and Giacomo Ferrari. 1983. Natural language input for scene generation. In *ACL Proceedings, First European Conference*, 175–182.

14. Adorni, Giovanni, Mauri Di Manzo and Fausto Giunchiglia. 1984. Natural language driven image generation. In *COLING-84*, 495–500.

15. Adorni, Giovanni, Mauri Di Manzo and Fausto Giunchiglia. 1984. Adaptive natural language generation. In *Artificial Intelligence and Information-Control Systems of Robots*, Ivan Plander, (ed.) North-Holland, Amsterdam, 77–80.

16. Adriaens, Geert. 1986. WEP (word expert parsing) revised and applied to Dutch. *ECAI-86* 1, 222–235.

17. Ahlswede, Thomas E. 1985. A linguistic string grammar of adjective definitions from Webster's Seventh Collegiate Dictionary. In *Humans and Machines: 4th Delaware Symposium on Language Studies*, Stephanie Williams, (ed.) Ablex, Norwood, 101–128.

18. Ahlswede, Thomas E. 1985. A tool kit for lexicon building. In *ACL Proceedings, 23rd Annual Meeting*, 268–276.

19. Ainon, Raja Noor. 1986. Storing text using integer codes. In *COLING-86*, 418–420.

20. Airenti, Gabriella, Bruno G. Bara and Marco Colombetti. 1984. Plan formation and failure recovery in communicative acts. In *ECAI-84*, 259–268.

21. Airenti, Gabriella, Bruno G. Bara and Marco Colombetti. 1984. Planning and understanding speech acts by interpersonal games. In *Computational Models of Natural Language Processing*, Bruno G. Bara and Giovanni Guida, (eds.) North-Holland, Amsterdam, 9–31.

22. Airenti, Gabriella, Bruno G. Bara and Marco Colombetti. 1985. Plan formation and failure recovery in communicative acts. In *Advances in Artificial Intelligence*, Tim O'Shea, (ed.) North-Holland, Amsterdam, 275–284.

23. Aizawa, Teruaki and Nobuko Hatada. 1980. Using a natural-artificial hybrid language for database access. In *COLING-80*, 543–549.

24. Akama, Seiki. 1986. Methodology and verifiability in Montague grammar. In *COLING-86*, 88–90.

25. Akama, Seiki and Masahito Kawamori. 1986. Situational investigation of presupposition. In *COLING-86*, 147–176.

26. Alam, Yukiko Sasaki. 1983. A two-level morphological analysis of Japanese. *Texas Linguistic Forum* 22, 229–252.

27. Ali, Yawar, Raymond Aubin and Barry Hall. 1986. A domain-independent natural language database interface. In *Proceedings of the 6th Canadian Conference on Artificial Intelligence*, 62–66.

28. Allen, James F. and C. Raymond Perrault. 1986 (1980). Analyzing intention in utterances. In *Readings in Natural Language Processing*, Barbara J. Grosz, Karen Sparck-Jones and Bonnie Lynn Webber, (eds.) Morgan Kaufmann, Los Altos, 441–458.

29. Allen, James F. and C. Raymond Perrault. 1980. Analyzing intention in utterances. *Artificial Intelligence* 15:3, 143–178.

30. Allen, James F. 1981. What's necessary to hide?: modeling action verbs. In *ACL Proceedings, 19th Annual Meeting*, 77–81.

31. Allen, James F., Alan M. Frisch and Diane J Litman. 1982. ARGOT: the Rochester dialogue system. In *AAAI-82*, 66–70.

32. Allen, James F. and Alan M Frisch. 1982. What's in a semantic network?. In *ACL Proceedings, 20th Annual Meeting*, 19–27.

33. Allen, James F. 1983. ARGOT: a system overview. *Computers and Mathematics with Applications* 9:1, 97–109.

34. Allen, James F. 1983. Recognizing intentions from natural language utterances. In *Computational Models of Discourse*, Michael Brady and Robert C. Berwick, (eds.) MIT Press, Cambridge, Ma., 107–166.

35. Allen, James F. 1984. Toward a general theory of action and time. *Artificial Intelligence* 23:2, 123–154.

36. Allen, Jonathan. 1982. Reflections on twenty years of the ACL. In *ACL Proceedings, 20th Annual Meeting*, 104–106.

37. Allen, Layman Edward. 1982. Towards a normalized language to clarify the structure of legal discourse. In *Deontic Logic, Computational Linguistics and Legal Information Systems*, Antonio A. Martino, (ed.) North-Holland, Amsterdam, 349–407.

38. Alshawi, Hiyan, Branimir K. Boguraev and Edward J Briscoe. 1985. Towards a dictionary support environment for real time parsing. In *ACL Proceedings, Second European Conference*, 171–178.

39. Alshawi, Hiyan. 1987. *Memory and Context for Language Interpretation*. Cambridge University Press, Cambridge.

40. Alterman, Richard. 1985. A dictionary based on concept coherence. *Artificial Intelligence* 25:2, 153–186.

41. Alterman, Richard. 1986. Summarization in the small. In *Advances in Cognitive Science 1*, Noel E. Sharkey, (ed.) Ellis Horwood/Wiley, Chichester/New York, 72–93.

42. Altmann, Gerry. 1985. The resolution of local syntactic ambiguity by the human sentence processing mechanism. In *ACL Proceedings, Second European Conference*, 123–127.

43. Amsler, Robert A. 1981. A taxonomy for English nouns and verbs. In *ACL Proceedings, 19th Annual Meeting*, 133–138.

44. Amsler, Robert A. 1984. Lexical knowledge bases. In *COLING-84*, 458–459.

45. Amsler, Robert A. 1987. Words and Worlds. In *TINLAP-3*, 16–19.

46. Anderson, John R. 1981. A theory of language acquisition based on general learning principles. *IJCAI-81* 1, 97–103.

47. Anderson, Lloyd B. 1984. Multilingual text-processing in a two-byte code: current issues. In *COLING-84*, 1–4.

48. Andersson, Annette O. 1986. A two-level description of written French. In *Papers from the Fifth Scandinavian Conference of Computational Linguistics*, Fred Karlsson, (ed.) University of Helsinki, Helsinki, 195–202.

49. Andre, Elizabeth, Guido Bosch, Gerd Herzog and Thomas Rist. 1986. Characterizing trajectories of moving objects using natural language path descriptions. *ECAI-86* 2, 1–8.

50. Andréka, H., T. Gergely and I Németi. 1980. Model theoretic semantics for many-purpose languages and language hierarchies. In *COLING-80*, 213–219.

51. Appelo, Lisette. 1986. A compositional approach to the translation of temporal expressions in the Rosetta system. In *COLING-86*, 313–318.

52. Appelt, Douglas E. 1986 (1985). Planning English referring expressions. In *Readings in Natural Language Processing*, Barbara J. Grosz, Karen Sparck-Jones and Bonnie Lynn Webber, (eds.) Morgan Kaufmann, Los Altos, 501–517.

53. Appelt, Douglas E. 1980. Problem solving applied to language generation. In *ACL Proceedings, 18th Annual Meeting*, 59–63.

54. Appelt, Douglas E. 1982. Planning natural-language utterances. In *AAAI-82*, 59–62.

55. Appelt, Douglas E. 1982. Planning natural language referring expressions. In *ACL Proceedings, 20th Annual Meeting*, 108–112.

56. Appelt, Douglas E. 1983. TELEGRAM: a grammar formalism for language planning. In *IJCAI-83*, 595–599.

57. Appelt, Douglas E. 1983. TELEGRAM: a grammar formalism for language parsing. In *ACL Proceedings, 21st Annual Meeting*, 74–78.

58. Appelt, Douglas E. 1985. Some pragmatic issues in the planning of definite and indefinite noun phrases. In *ACL Proceedings, 23rd Annual Meeting*, 198–203.

59. Appelt, Douglas E. 1985. Planning English referring expressions. *Artificial Intelligence* 26:1, 1–34.

60. Appelt, Douglas E. and Amichai Kronfeld. 1987. A computational model of referring. *IJCAI-87* 2, 640–647.

61. Appelt, Douglas E. 1987. Reference and pragmatic identification. In *TINLAP-3*, 128–132.

62. Appelt, Douglas E. 1987. Bidirectional grammars and the design of natural language generation systems. In *TINLAP-3*, 185–191.

63. Appelt, Dougls E. 1985. *Planning English Sentences*. Cambridge University Press, Cambridge.

64. Arens, Yigal. 1981. Using language and context in the analysis of text. *IJCAI-81* 1, 52–57.

65. Arens, Yigal, John. J. Granacki and Alice C Parker. 1987. Phrasal analysis of multi-noun sequences. In *ACL Proceedings, 25th Annual Meeting*, 59–64.

66. Arnold, Doug and Louis des Tombe. 1987. Basic theory and methodology in EUROTRA. In *Machine Translation: Theoretical and Methodological Issues*, Sergei Nirenberg, (ed.) Cambridge University Press, Cambridge, 114–135.

67. Arnold, Doug J. and Rod L Johnson. 1984. Robust processing in machine translation. In *COLING-84*, 472–475.

68. Arnold, Doug J., Steven Krauwer, Michael A. Rosner, Louis des Tombe and G.B Varile. 1986. The <C,A>T framework in EUROTRA: a theoretically committed notation for MT. In *COLING-86*, 297–303.

69. August, Stephanie E. and Michael G Dyer. 1985. Understanding analogies in editorials. *IJCAI-85* 2, 845–847.

70. Ayuso, Damaris, Varda Shaked and Ralph Weischedel. 1987. An environment for acquiring semantic information. In *ACL Proceedings, 25th Annual Meeting*, 32–40.

71. Bachenko, Joan, Donald Hindle and Eileen Fitzpatrick. 1983. Constraining a deterministic parser. In *AAAI-83*, 8–11.

72. Bachenko, Joan, Eileen Fitzpatrick and C.E Wright. 1986. The contribution of parsing to prosody in an experimental text-to-speech synthesis. In *ACL Proceedings, 24th Annual Meeting*, 145–155.

73. Bachut, Daniel and Nelson Verastegui. 1984. Software tools for the environment of a computer aided translation system. In *COLING-84*, 330–333.

74. Bailes, P.A.C. and L.H Reeker. 1980. An experimental applicative programming language for linguistics and string processing. In *COLING-80*, 520–525.

75. Bainbridge, R.I. 1985. Montagovian definite clause grammar. In *ACL Proceedings, Second European Conference*, 25–34.

76. Bainbridge, Stewart and Douglas Skuce. 1980. Knowledge Acquisition and representation using logic, set theory and natural language structures. In *Proceedings of the Third Biennial Conference of the Canadian Society for Computational Studies of Intelligence (3rd Canadian Conference on AI)*, 296–303.

77. Bakel, Jan van. 1984. *Automatic Semantic Interpretation: A Computer Model of Understanding Language*. Foris, Dordrecht.

78. Ballard, Bruce W. 1984. The syntax and semantics of user-defined modifiers in a transportable natural language processor. In *COLING-84*, 52–56.

79. Ballard, Bruce W. and Nancy L Tinkham. 1984. A phrase-structured grammatical framework for transportable natural language processing. *Computational Linguistics* 10:2, 81–96.

80. Ballard, Bruce W. 1986. User specification of syntactic case frames in TELI, a transportable, user-customized natural language processor. In *COLING-86*, 454–460.

81. Ballard, Bruce W. and Douglas Stumberger. 1986. Semantic acquisition in TELI: a transportable user-customized natural language processor. In *ACL Proceedings, 24th Annual Meeting*, 20–29.

82. Bara, Bruno G. and Giovanni Guida, (eds.) 1984. *Computational Models of Natural Language Processing*. North-Holland, Amsterdam.

83. Bara, Bruno G. and Giovanni Guida. 1984. Competence and performance in the design of natural language systems. In *Computational Models of Natural Language Processing*, Bruno G. Bara and Giovanni Guida, (eds.) North-Holland, Amsterdam, 1–7.

84. Barnett, Brigitte, Hubert Lehmann and Magdalena Zoeppritz. 1986. A word database for natural language processing. In *COLING-86*, 435–440.

85. Baron, Naomi S. 1986. Language, sublanguage, and the promise of machine translation. *Computers and Translation* 1:1, 3–20.

86. Barr, Avron and Edward A. Feigenbaum, (eds.) 1981. *The Handbook of Artificial Intelligence*. vol. 1, William Kaufmann., Palo Alto.

87. Barton, G. Edward, Jr. and Robert C Berwick. 1985. Parsing with assertion sets and information monotonicity. *IJCAI-85* 2, 769–771.

88. Barton, G. Edward, Jr. 1985. The computational difficulty of ID/LP parsing. In *ACL Proceedings, 23rd Annual Meeting*, 76–81.

89. Barton, G. Edward, Jr. 1985. On the complexity of ID/LP parsing. *Computational Linguistics* 11:4, 205–218.

90. Barton, G. Edward, Jr. 1986. Constraint propagation in Kimmo systems. In *ACL Proceedings, 24th Annual Meeting*, 45–52.

91. Barton, G. Edward, Jr. 1986. Computational complexity in two-level morphology. In *ACL Proceedings, 24th Annual Meeting*, 53–59.

92. Barton, G. Edward Jr., Robert C. Berwick and Eric Sven Ristad. 1987. *Computational Complexity and Natural Language*. MIT Press, Cambridge, Ma..

93. Barwise, Jon. 1981. Some computational aspects of situation semantics. In *ACL Proceedings, 19th Annual Meeting*, 109–111.

94. Bates, Madeleine and Robert Ingria. 1981. Controlled transformational sentence generation. In *ACL Proceedings, 19th Annual Meeting*, 153–158.

95. Bates, Madeleine. 1984. There is still gold in the database mine. In *COLING-84*, 184–185.

96. Bauer-Bernet, Hélène. 1982. Legal thesauri and data processing. In *Deontic Logic, Computational Linguistics and Legal Information Systems*, Antonio A. Martino, (ed.) North-Holland, Amsterdam, 237–266.

97. Bayer, Samuel, Leonard Joseph and Candace Kalish. 1985. Grammatical relations as the basis for natural language parsing and text understanding. *IJCAI-85* 2, 788–790.

98. Bayer, Samuel. 1986. A relational representation of modification. *AAAI-86* 2, 1074–1078.

99. Beale, Andrew D. 1985. A probabilistic approach to grammatical analysis of written English by computer. In *ACL Proceedings, Second European Conference*, 159–165.

100. Beale, Andrew D. 1985. Grammatical analysis by computer of the Lancaster-Oslo/Bergen (LOB) corpus of British English texts. In *ACL Proceedings, 23rd Annual Meeting*, 293–298.

101. Bear, John. 1983. A breadth-first parsing model. In *IJCAI-83*, 696–698.

102. Bear, John. 1986. A morphological recognizer with syntactic and phonological rules. In *COLING-86*, 272–276.

103. Becker, Lee A. 1981. PHONY: a heuristic phonological analyzer. In *ACL Proceedings, 19th Annual Meeting*, 23–28.

104. Beckman, Mary E. and Janet B Pierrehumbert. 1986. Japanese prosodic phrasing and intonation synthesis. In *ACL Proceedings, 24th Annual Meeting*, 173–180.

105. Beesley, Kenneth R. and David Hefner. 1986. PeriPhrase: Lingware for parsing and structural transfer. In *COLING-86*, 390–392.

106. Begier, B. 1982. Knowledge representation method based on predicate calculus in an intelligent CAI system. In *COLING-82*, 13–18.

107. Bennett, Paul A., Rod L. Johnson, John McNaught, Jeanette Pugh, J.C. Sager and Harold L Somers. 1986. *Multilingual Aspects of Information Technology*. Gower, Aldershot.

108. Berendsen, Egon, Simone Langeweg and Hugo Van Leuven. 1986. Computational phonology: merged, not mixed. In *COLING-86*, 612–614.

109. Bernstein, Jared and Larry Nessly. 1981. Performance comparison of component algorithms for phonemicization of orthography. In *ACL Proceedings, 19th Annual Meeting*, 19–22.

110. Beroule, Dominique. 1983. Vocal interface for a man-machine dialog. In *ACL Proceedings, First European Conference*, 43–48.

111. Berry-Rogghe, Genevieve L., Monika Kolvenbach and Hans-Dieter Lutz. 1980. Interacting with PLIDIS, a deductive question answering system for German. In *Natural Language Question Answering Systems*, Leonard Bolc, (ed.) Hanser, Munich, 137–216.

112. Berry-Rogghe, Genevieve L. 1985. Interpreting singular definite descriptions in database queries. In *ACL Proceedings, Second European Conference*, 213–217.

113. Berthelin, J.B. 1980. Connotation as a form of inference. In *COLING-80*, 228–235.

114. Berwick, Robert C. 1980. Computational Analogues of constraints on grammars: a model of syntactic acquisition. In *ACL Proceedings, 18th Annual Meeting*, 49–53.

115. Berwick, Robert C. 1981. Computational complexity and lexical functional grammar. In *ACL Proceedings, 19th Annual Meeting*, 7–12.

116. Berwick, Robert C. and Kenneth Wexler. 1982. Parsing efficiency, binding, and C-command. In *Proceedings of the Fifth West Coast Conference on Formal Linguistics*, Daniel P. Flickinger, Marlys Macken and Nancy Wiegand, (eds.) Stanford Linguistics Association, Stanford, 41–52.

117. Berwick, Robert C. and Amy S Weinberg. 1982. Parsing efficiency, computational complexity, and the evaluation of grammatical theories. *Linguistic Inquiry* 13:2, 165–191.

118. Berwick, Robert C. 1982. Computational complexity and lexical-functional grammar. *American Journal of Computational Linguistics* 8:3–4, 97–109.

119. Berwick, Robert C. 1983. A deterministic parser with broad coverage. In *IJCAI-83*, 710–712.

120. Berwick, Robert C. and Amy S Weinberg. 1983. Syntactic constraints and efficient parsability. In *ACL Proceedings, 21st Annual Meeting*, 119–122.

121. Berwick, Robert C. 1983. Computational aspects of discourse. In *Computational Models of Discourse*, Michael Brady and Robert C. Berwick, (eds.) MIT Press, Cambridge, Ma., 27–105.

122. Berwick, Robert C. 1984. Bounded context parsing and easy learnability. In *COLING-84*, 20–23.

123. Berwick, Robert C. 1984. Strong generative capacity, weak generative capacity, and modern linguistic theories. *Computational Linguistics* 10:3–4, 189–202.

124. Berwick, Robert C. and Samuel F Pilato. 1985. Reversible automata and induction of the English auxiliary system. *IJCAI-85* 2, 880–882.

125. Berwick, Robert C. and Sandiway Fong. 1985. New approaches to parsing conjunctions using PROLOG. In *ACL Proceedings, 23rd Annual Meeting*, 118–126.

126. Berwick, Robert C. and Candace L Sidner. 1986. *Tutorial Syllabus no. 18: Natural Language Processing*. AAAI, Menlo Park.

127. Berwick, Robert C. 1987. Intelligent natural language processing. In *AI in the 1980s and Beyond: An MIT Survey*, W. Eric L. Grimson and Ramesh S. Patil, (eds.) MIT Press, Cambridge, Ma., 00–00.

128. Besemer, David J. and Paul S Jacobs. 1987. FLUSH: a flexible logic design. In *ACL Proceedings, 25th Annual Meeting*, 186–192.

129. Bestougeff, Helene and Gerard Ligozat. 1984. Processing tense information in French utterances. In *ECAI-84*, 209–212.

130. Bestougeff, Helene and Gerard Ligozat. 1985. Parametrized abstract objects for linguistic information processing. In *ACL Proceedings, Second European Conference*, 107–115.

131. Biber, Douglas. 1985. Investigating macroscopic textual variation through multifeature/ multidimensional analyses. *Linguistics* 23:2, 337–360.

132. Bień, Janusz S., Krystyna Laus-Macyńska and Stanislaw Szpakowicz. 1980. Parsing free word order languages in PROLOG. In *COLING-80*, 346–349.

133. Bień, Janusz S. 1983. Articles and resource control. In *IJCAI-83*, 675–677.

134. Bień, Janusz S. 1985. Experiments in parsing Polish. In *Proceedings of an International Workshop on Natural Language Understanding and Logic Programming, University of Rennes*.

135. Biermann, Alan W. and Bruce W Ballard. 1980. Toward natural language computation. *American Journal of Computational Linguistics* 6:2, 71–86.

136. Biermann, Alan W., R. Rodman, Bruce W. Ballard, T. Betancourt, G. Bilbro, H. Deas, L. Fineman, P. Fink, D. Gregory, K. Gilbert and F Heidlage. 1983. Interactive natural language processing: a pragmatic approach. In *ACL Proceedings, Conference on Applied Natural Language Processing*, 180–191.

137. Binot, Jean-Louis, M. Graitson, Ph. Lemaire and Daniel Ribbens. 1980. Automatic processing of written French language. In *COLING-80*, 9–14.

138. Binot, Jean-Louis. 1984. A set-oriented semantic network formalism for the representation of sentence meaning. In *ECAI-84*, 147–156.

139. Binot, Jean-Louis. 1985. A set-oriented semantic network formalism for the representation of sentence meaning. In *Advances in Artificial Intelligence*, Tim O'Shea, (ed.) North-Holland, Amsterdam, 305–314.

140. Binot, Jean-Louis and Daniel Ribbens. 1986. Dual frames: a new tool for semantic parsing. *AAAI-86* 1, 579–583.

141. Binot, Jean-Louis and Karen Jensen. 1987. A semantic expert using an online standard dictionary. *IJCAI-87* 2, 709–714.

142. Birnbaum, Lawrence, Margot Flowers and Rod McGuire. 1980. Towards an AI model of argumentation. In *AAAI-80*, 313–315.

143. Birnbaum, Lawrence and Mallory Selfridge. 1981. Conceptual analysis of natural language. In *Inside Computer Understanding: Five Programs plus Miniatures*, Roger C. Schank and Christopher K. Riesbeck, (eds.) Erlbaum, Hillsdale, 318–353.

144. Birnbaum, Lawrence and Mallory Selfridge. 1981. Micro ELI. In *Inside Computer Understanding: Five Programs plus Miniatures*, Roger C. Schank and Christopher K. Riesbeck, (eds.) Erlbaum, Hillsdale, 354–372.

145. Birnbaum, Lawrence. 1982. Argument molecules: a functional representation of argument structure. In *AAAI-82*, 63–65.

146. Birnbaum, Lawrence. 1985. Lexical ambiguity as a touchstone for theories of language analysis. *IJCAI-85* 2, 815–820.

147. Birnbaum, Lawrence. 1987. Let's put the AI back in NLP. In *TINLAP-3*, 00–00.

148. Blank, Glenn D. 1985. A new kind of finite-state automation: register vector grammar. *IJCAI-85* 2, 749–755.

149. Blåberg, Olli. 1985. A two-level description of Swedish. In *Computational Morphosyntax: Report on Research 1981–1984*, Fred Karlsson, (ed.) University of Helsinki, Helsinki, 43–62.

150. Block, Hans-Ulrich and Hans Haugeneder. 1986. The treatment of movement-rules in a LFG-parser. In *COLING-86*, 482–486.

151. Block, Hans-Ulrich and Rudolf Hunze. 1986. Incremental construction of C- and F-structure in a LFG-parser. In *COLING-86*, 490–493.

152. Blois, Marsden S., David D. Sherertz and Mark S Tuttle. 1980. Word and object in disease descriptions. In *ACL Proceedings, 18th Annual Meeting*, 149–152.

153. Bobrow, Danny and the PARC Understander Group. 1986 (1979). GUS, a frame driven dialog system. In *Readings in Natural Language Processing*, Barbara J. Grosz, Karen Sparck-Jones and Bonnie Lynn Webber, (eds.) Morgan Kaufmann, Los Altos, 595–604.

154. Bobrow, Robert J. and Bonnie Lynn Webber. 1980. PSI-KLONE. In *Proceedings of the Third Biennial Conference of the Canadian Society for Computational Studies of Intelligence (3rd Canadian Conference on AI)*, 131–142.

155. Bobrow, Robert J. and Bonnie Lynn Webber. 1980. Knowledge representation for syntactic/semantic processing. In *AAAI-80*, 316–323.

156. Bobrow, Robert J. and Bonnie Lynn Webber. 1981. Some issues in parsing and natural language understanding. In *ACL Proceedings, 19th Annual Meeting*, 97–99.

157. Bobrow, Robert J. and Madeleine Bates. 1982. Design dimensions for non-normative understanding systems. In *ACL Proceedings, 20th Annual Meeting*, 153–156.

158. Boguraev, Branimir K. and Karen Sparck-Jones. 1981. A general semantic analyzer for data base access. *IJCAI-81* 1, 443–445.

159. Boguraev, Branimir K. and Karen Sparck-Jones. 1982. Steps towards natural language to data language translation using general semantic information. In *ECAI-82*, 232–233.

160. Boguraev, Branimir K. 1983. Recognising conjunctions within the ATN framework. In *Automatic Natural Language Parsing*, Karen Sparck-Jones and Yorick A. Wilks, (eds.) Ellis Horwood/Wiley, Chichester/New York, 39–45.

161. Boguraev, Branimir K. and Karen Sparck-Jones. 1983. How to drive a database front end using general semantic information. In *ACL Proceedings, Conference on Applied Natural Language Processing*, 81–88.

162. Boguraev, Branimir K. 1987. The definitional power of words. In *TINLAP-3*, 11–15.

163. Boguraev, Branimir K., Edward J. Briscoe, John Carroll, David Carter and Claire Grover. 1987. The derivation of grammatically indexed lexicon from the Longman Dictionary of Contemporary English. In *ACL Proceedings, 25th Annual Meeting*, 193–200.

164. Boitet, Christian, P. Chatelin and P. Daun Fraga. 1980. Present and future paradigms in the automatized translation of natural languages. In *COLING-80*, 430–436.

165. Boitet, Christian and Nikolai Nedobejkine. 1980. Russian-French at GETA: outline of the method and detailed example. In *COLING-80*, 437–446.

166. Boitet, Christian and Nikolai Nedobejkine. 1981. Recent developments in Russian-French machine translation at Grenoble. *Linguistics* 19:3/4, 199–271.

167. Boitet, Christian, P. Guillaume and M Quezel-Ambrunaz. 1982. Implementation and conversational environment of ARIANE 78.4: an integrated system for automated translation and human revision. In *COLING-82*, 19–27.

168. Boitet, Christian and René Gerber. 1984. Expert systems and other techniques in MT system. In *COLING-84*, 468–471.

169. Boitet, Christian, Nelson Verastegui and Daniel Bachut. 1985. Various representations of text proposed for EUROTRA. In *ACL Proceedings, Second European Conference*, 73–78.

170. Boitet, Christian and Nikolai Nedobejkine. 1986. Toward integrated dictionaries for M(a)T: motivations and linguistic organisation. In *COLING-86*, 423–428.

171. Bolc, Leonard, (ed.) 1980. *Natural Language Based Computer Systems*. Hanser, Munich.

172. Bolc, Leonard, (ed.) 1980. *Natural Language Question Answering Systems*. Hanser, Munich.

173. Bolc, Leonard, (ed.) 1980. *Representation and Processing of Natural Language*. Hanser, Munich.

174. Bolc, Leonard and Tomek Strzalkowski. 1982. Transformation of natural language into logical formulas. In *COLING-82*, 29–35.

175. Bolc, Leonard and P Strzalkowski. 1982. Transformation of medical text into a deductive data base. In *Proceedings of the 7th ALLC Symposium on Computers in Literary and Linguistic Research*.

176. Bolc, Leonard, K. Kochut, A. Lesniewski and Tomek Strzalkowski. 1983. Natural language information retrieval dialog. In *ACL Proceedings, First European Conference*, 196–203.

177. Bolc, Leonard, K. Kochut, A. Kowalski and M Kozlowska. 1984. Natural language information retrieval system with extension towards fuzzy reasoning in medicine. In *ECAI-84*, 230.

178. Bolc, Leonard. 1984. Deductive question answering system Dialog. In *Artificial Intelligence and Information-Control Systems of Robots*, I. Plander, (ed.) Elsevier.

179. Bolc, Leonard, K. Kochut, P. Rychlik and Tomek Strzalkowski. 1984. Deductive question answering system DIALOG. In *Artificial Intelligence and Information-Control Systems of Robots*, Ivan Plander, (ed.) North-Holland, Amsterdam, 17–24.

180. Bookman, Lawrence A. 1987. A microfeature-based scheme for modelling semantics. *IJCAI-87* 2, 611–614.

181. Borghesi, L. and C Favareto. 1982. Flexible parsing of discretely uttered sentences. In *COLING-82*, 37–42.

182. Borin, Lars. 1986. What is a lexical representation?. In *Papers from the Fifth Scandinavian Conference of Computational Linguistics*, Fred Karlsson, (ed.) University of Helsinki, Helsinki, 25–34.

183. Boyer, Michel and Guy Lapalme. 1985. Generating sentences from semantic networks. In *Natural Language Understanding and Logic Programming*, Veronica Dahl and Patrick Saint-Dizier, (eds.) North-Holland, Amsterdam, 181–189.

184. Boyer, Michel and Guy Lapalme. 1985. Generating paraphrases from meaning-text semantic networks. *Computational Intelligence* 1:3 and 4, 103–117.

185. Bradford, J. 1982. A metric space defined on English and its relation to error correction. In *COLING-82*, 43–48.

186. Brady, Michael and Robert C. Berwick, (eds.) 1983. *Computational Models of Discourse.*. MIT Press, Cambridge, Ma..

187. Brennan, Susan E., Marilyn W. Friedman and Carl Pollard. 1987. A centering approach to pronouns. In *ACL Proceedings, 25th Annual Meeting*, 155–162.

188. Brewer, William F. 1982. Plan understanding, narrative comprehension, and story schemas. In *AAAI-82*, 262–264.

189. Brée, D. S., R. A. Smit and H. P. Schotel. 1984. Generation and comprehension of Dutch subordinating conjunctions by computer. In *ECAI-84*, 205–208.

190. Brée, D. S. and R. A. Smit. 1985. Non-standard uses of 'if'. In *ACL Proceedings, Second European Conference*, 218–225.

191. Brée, D. S. and R. A. Smit. 1986. Linking propositions. In *COLING-86*, 177–180.

192. Brietzmann, Astrid and Guenther Goerz. 1982. Pragmatics in speech understanding - revisited. In *COLING-82*, 49–54.

193. Brietzmann, Astrid and Ute Ehrlich. 1986. The role of semantic processing in an automatic speech understanding system. In *COLING-86*, 596–598.

194. Brinkmann, Karl-Heinz. 1980. Terminology data banks as a basis for high-quality translation. In *COLING-80*, 463.

195. Briscoe, Edward J. 1983. Determinism and its implementation in PARSIFAL. In *Automatic Natural Language Parsing*, Karen Sparck-Jones and Yorick A. Wilks, (eds.) Ellis Horwood/Wiley, Chichester/New York, 61–68.

196. Briscoe, Edward J. and Branimir K Boguraev. 1984. Control structures and theories of interaction in speech understanding systems. In *COLING-84*, 259–266.

197. Briscoe, Edward J., Claire Grover, Branimir K. Boguraev and John Carroll. 1987. A formalism and environment for the development of a large grammar of English. *IJCAI-87* 2, 703–708.

198. Brodda, Benny. 1983. An experiment with heuristic parsing of Swedish. In *ACL Proceedings, First European Conference*, 66–73.

199. Brodda, Benny. 1986. BetaText: an event driven text processing and text analyzing system. In *COLING-86*, 421–422.

200. Bronnenberg, W.J.H.J., Harry C. Bunt, S.P. Jan Landsbergen, Remko J.H. Scha, W.J. Schoenmakers and E.P.C. van Utteren. 1980. The question answering system PHLIQA1. In *Natural Language Question Answering Systems*, Leonard Bolc, (ed.) Hanser, Munich, 217–305.

201. Brotsky, Daniel C. and Charles Rich. 1985. Issues in the design of hybrid knowledge representation and reasoning systems. In *Theoretical Approaches to Natural Language Understanding, a Workshop at Halifax, Nova Scotia*, 32–38.

202. Brown, F.M. and Camilla B Schwind. 1980. An integrated theory of natural language understanding. In *Representation and Processing of Natural Language*, Leonard Bolc, (ed.) Hanser, Munich, 85–120.

203. Brown, Gretchen P. 1980. Characterizing indirect speech acts. *American Journal of Computational Linguistics* 6:3–4, 150–166.

204. Bruce, Bertram C. 1986 (1975). Generation as a social action. In *Readings in Natural Language Processing*, Barbara J. Grosz, Karen Sparck-Jones and Bonnie Lynn Webber, (eds.) Morgan Kaufmann, Los Altos, 419–422.

205. Bruce, Bertram C. 1982. Natural communication between person and computer. In *Strategies for Natural Language Processing*, Wendy G. Lehnert and Martin H. Ringle, (eds.) Erlbaum, Hillsdale, 55–88.

206. Bruce, Bertram C. 1983. Belief systems and language understanding. In *Computers in Language Research 2*, Walter A. Sedelow, Jr. and Sally Yeates Sedelow, (eds.) Trends in Linguistics, Walter de Gruyter & Co., Berlin, 113–160.

207. Bryant, Barret R., Dale Johnson and Balanjaninath Edupuganty. 1986. Formal specification of natural language syntax using two-level grammar. In *COLING-86*, 527–532.

208. Buchmann, Beat, Susan Warwick and Patrick Shann. 1984. Design of a machine translation system for a sublanguage. In *COLING-84*, 334–337.

209. Bukowski, Jedrzej. 1986. Indexage lexical au GETA. In *COLING-86*, 429–431.

210. Bunt, Harry C. 1984. The resolution of quantificational ambiguities in the TENDUM computational linguistics research system. In *COLING-84*, 130–133.

211. Burton, Richard R. and John S Brown. 1986 (1979). Toward a natural language capability for computer-aided instruction. In *Readings in Natural Language Processing*, Barbara J. Grosz, Karen Sparck-Jones and Bonnie Lynn Webber, (eds.) Morgan Kaufmann, Los Altos, 605–625.

212. Busemann, Stephan. 1984. Topicalization and pronominalization: extending a natural language generation system. In *ECAI-84*, 221–224.

213. Butler, Christopher. 1985. *Computers in Linguistics*. Blackwell, Oxford.

214. Byrd, Roy J. 1983. Word formation in natural language processing systems. In *IJCAI-83*, 704–706.

215. Byrd, Roy J. and Martin S Chodorow. 1985. Using an on-line dictionary to find rhyming words and pronunciations for unknown words. In *ACL Proceedings, 23rd Annual Meeting*, 277–283.

216. Byrd, Roy J., Judith L. Klavans, Mark Aronoff and Frank Anshen. 1986. Computer methods for morphological analysis. In *ACL Proceedings, 24th Annual Meeting*, 120–127.

217. Calzolari, Nicoletta. 1984. Detecting patterns in a lexical data base. In *COLING-84*, 170–173.

218. Calzolari, Nicoletta. 1984. Machine-readable dictionaries, lexical data bases and the lexical system. In *COLING-84*, 460.

219. Cappelli, Amedeo, Giacomo Ferrari, Lorenzo Moretti, Irina Prodanof and Oliviero Stock. 1980. Automatic analysis of Italian. In *AISB-80*, 46–51.

220. Cappelli, Amedeo and Lorenzo Moretti. 1983. An approach to natural language in the SI-nets paradigm. In *ACL Proceedings, First European Conference*, 122–128.

221. Cappelli, Amedeo, Giacomo Ferrari, Lorenzo Moretti and Irina Prodanoff. 1984. A framework for integrating syntax and semantics. In *Computational Models of Natural Language Processing*, Bruno G. Bara and Giovanni Guida, (eds.) North-Holland, Amsterdam, 33–57.

222. Carberry, Sandra. 1983. Tracking user goals in an information-seeking environment. In *AAAI-83*, 59–63.

223. Carberry, Sandra. 1984. Understanding pragmatically ill-formed input. In *COLING-84*, 200–206.

224. Carberry, Sandra. 1985. A pragmatics-based approach to understanding intersentential ellipsis. In *ACL Proceedings, 23rd Annual Meeting*, 188–197.

225. Carberry, Sandra. 1986. User models: the problem of disparity. In *COLING-86*, 29–34.

226. Carberry, Sandra. 1986. TRACK: Toward a robust natural language interface. In *Proceedings of the 6th Canadian Conference on Artificial Intelligence*, 84–88.

227. Carbonell, Jaime G. 1980. Metaphor - a key to extensible semantic analysis. In *ACL Proceedings, 18th Annual Meeting*, 17–21.

228. Carbonell, Jaime G. 1980. Towards a process model of human personality traits. *Artificial Intelligence* 15:1,2, 49–74.

229. Carbonell, Jaime G. 1981. POLITICS. In *Inside Computer Understanding: Five Programs plus Miniatures*, Roger C. Schank and Christopher K. Riesbeck, (eds.) Erlbaum, Hillsdale, 259–307.

230. Carbonell, Jaime G. 1981. Micro POLITICS. In *Inside Computer Understanding: Five Programs plus Miniatures*, Roger C. Schank and Christopher K. Riesbeck, (eds.) Erlbaum, Hillsdale, 308–317.

231. Carbonell, Jaime G. and Philip J Hayes. 1981. Dynamic strategy selection in flexible parsing. In *ACL Proceedings, 19th Annual Meeting*, 143–147.

232. Carbonell, Jaime G. 1982. Metaphor: an inescapable phenomenon. In *Strategies for Natural Language Processing*, Wendy G. Lehnert and Martin H. Ringle, (eds.) Erlbaum, Hillsdale, 415–434.

233. Carbonell, Jaime G., W. Mark Boggs, Michael L. Mauldin and Peter G Anick. 1983. The XCALIBUR project: a natural language interface to expert systems. In *IJCAI-83*, 653–656.

234. Carbonell, Jaime G. 1983. Discourse pragmatics in task-oriented natural language interfaces. In *ACL Proceedings, 21st Annual Meeting*, 164–168.

235. Carbonell, Jaime G. and Philip J Hayes. 1983. Recovery strategies for parsing extragrammatical language. *American Journal of Computational Linguistics* 9:3–4, 123–146.

236. Carbonell, Jaime G. 1984. Is there natural language after databases?. In *COLING-84*, 186–187.

237. Carbonell, Jaime G. and Philip J Hayes. 1984. Coping with extragrammaticality. In *COLING-84*, 437–443.

238. Carbonell, Jaime G. 1986. Requirements for robust natural language interfaces: the LanguageCraft (TM) and XCALIBUR experiences. In *COLING-86*, 162–163.

239. Carbonell, Jaime G. and Masaru Tomita. 1987. Knowledge based machine translation, the CMU approach. In *Machine Translation: Theoretical and Methodological Issues*, Sergei Nirenberg, (ed.) Cambridge University Press, Cambridge, 68–89.

240. Carey, John. 1980. Paralanguage in computer mediated communication. In *ACL Proceedings, 18th Annual Meeting*, 67–69.

241. Carlson, Lauri. 1986. LP rules in unification grammar. In *Papers from the Fifth Scandinavian Conference of Computational Linguistics*, Fred Karlsson, (ed.) University of Helsinki, Helsinki, 35–48.

242. Carroll, John. 1983. An island parsing interpreter for the full augmented transition network formalism. In *ACL Proceedings, First European Conference*, 101–105.

243. Carter, Alan W. and Michael J Freiling. 1984. Simplifying deterministic parsing. In *COLING-84*, 239–242.

244. Carter, David M. 1984. An approach to general machine translation based on preference semantics and local focussing. In *ECAI-84*, 231.

245. Castelfranchi, Cristiano, Domenico Parisi and Oliviero Stock. 1984. Knowledge representation and natural language: extending the expressive power of proposition nodes. In *Computational Models of Natural Language Processing*, Bruno G. Bara and Giovanni Guida, (eds.) North-Holland, Amsterdam, 59–89.

246. Cater, Arthur W.S. 1980. Analysing English text: a non-deterministic approach with limited memory. In *AISB-80*, 52–65.

247. Cater, Arthur W.S. 1983. Request-based parsing with low-level syntactic recognition. In *Automatic Natural Language Parsing*, Karen Sparck-Jones and Yorick A. Wilks, (eds.) Ellis Horwood/Wiley, Chichester/New York, 141–147.

248. Cater, Arthur W.S. 1986. Preference-directed use of ATNs. *ECAI-86* 2, 23–28.

249. Cercone, Nick. 1980. The representation and use of knowledge in an associative network for the automatic comprehension of natural language. In *Representation and Processing of Natural Language*, Leonard Bolc, (ed.) Hanser, Munich, 121–205.

250. Cercone, Nick, Max Krause and John Boates. 1983. Minimal and almost minimal perfect hash function search with application to natural language lexicon design. *Computers and Mathematics with Applications* 9:1, 215–231.

251. Cercone, Nick and Gordon I McCalla. 1986. Accessing knowledge through natural language. In *Advances in Computers*, Marshall C. Yovits, (ed.) vol. 25, Academic Press, New York, 00–00.

252. Cerri, Stefano A. and J Breuker. 1980. A rather intelligent language teacher. In *AISB-80*, 66–70.

253. Cerri, Stefano A. and Marie-France Merger. 1983. Learning translation skills with a knowledge-based tutor: French-Italian conjunctions in context. In *ACL Proceedings, First European Conference*, 133–138.

254. Chafe, Wallace. 1980. Should computers write spoken language ?. In *ACL Proceedings, 18th Annual Meeting*, 27–28.

255. Chan, Chorkin. 1980. A Chinese characters coding scheme for computer input and internal storage. In *COLING-80*, 274–278.

256. Chapin, Paul G. 1982. ACL in 1977. In *ACL Proceedings, 20th Annual Meeting*, 103.

257. Charniak, Eugene. 1986 (1973). Jack and Jane in search of a theory of knowledge. In *Readings in Natural Language Processing*, Barbara J. Grosz, Karen Sparck-Jones and Bonnie Lynn Webber, (eds.) Morgan Kaufmann, Los Altos, 331–337.

258. Charniak, Eugene. 1981. The case-slot identity theory. *Cognitive Science* 5:3, 285–292.

259. Charniak, Eugene. 1981. Six topics in search of a parser: an overview of AI language research. *IJCAI-81* 2, 1079–1087.

260. Charniak, Eugene. 1981. A common representation for problem-solving and language-comprehension information. *Artificial Intelligence* 16:3, 225–256.

261. Charniak, Eugene. 1982. Context recognition in language comprehension. In *Strategies for Natural Language Processing*, Wendy G. Lehnert and Martin H. Ringle, (eds.) Erlbaum, Hillsdale, 435–454.

262. Charniak, Eugene. 1983. Passing markers: a theory of contextual influence in language comprehension. *Cognitive Science* 7:3, 171–190.

263. Charniak, Eugene. 1983. A parser with something for everyone. In *Parsing Natural Language*, Margaret King, (ed.) Academic Press, London, 117–149.

264. Charniak, Eugene. 1983. Parsing, how to. In *Automatic Natural Language Parsing*, Karen Sparck-Jones and Yorick A. Wilks, (eds.) Ellis Horwood/Wiley, Chichester/New York, 156–163.

265. Charniak, Eugene. 1986. A neat theory of marker passing. *AAAI-86* 1, 584–588.

266. Charniak, Eugene and Mitchell P Marcus. 1986. *Tutorial Syllabus no. 9: Natural Language Processing.* AAAI, Menlo Park.

267. Charniak, Eugene. 1987. Connectionism and explanation. In *TINLAP-3*, 00–00.

268. Chauché, J. 1984. Un outil multidimensionnel de l'analyse du discours. In *COLING-84*, 11–15.

269. Chauché, J. 1986. Déduction automatiques et systèmes transformationnels. In *COLING-86*, 408–411.

270. Chester, Daniel. 1980. A parsing algorithm that extends phrases. *American Journal of Computational Linguistics* 6:2, 87–96.

271. Chester, Daniel. 1985. Towards a natural language semantics formalized in terms of physical symbol systems. In *Humans and Machines: 4th Delaware Symposium on Language Studies*, Stephanie Williams, (ed.) Ablex, Norwood, 54–66.

272. Chin, David N. 1983. Knowledge structures in UC, the UNIX consultant. In *ACL Proceedings, 21st Annual Meeting*, 159–163.

273. Chodorow, Martin S., Roy J. Byrd and George E Heidorn. 1985. Extracting semantic hierarchies form a large on-line dictionary. In *ACL Proceedings, 23rd Annual Meeting*, 299–304.

274. Choi, J.M., M.S. Song, K.J. Jeong, H.C. Kwon, S.Y. Han and Y.T Kim. 1985. A PROLOG-based Korean-English machine translation system and its efficient method of dictionary management. In *Logic Programming '85: Proceedings of the 4th Conference, Tokyo*, Eiiti Wada, (ed.) Springer, Berlin, 236–245.

275. Choi, Key-Sun and Gil Chan Kim. 1983. Parsing Korean based on revised PTQ. In *Proceedings of the Second Japanese-Korean Joint Workshop on Formal Grammar*, Arata Ishimoto, Shogo Inokuchi, Ken-ichi Murata and Akira Ikeya, (eds.) Logico-Linguistic Society of Japan, Kyoto, 59–76.

276. Choi, Key-Sun. 1984. Petri net grammars for natural language analysis. *Language Research* 20:2, 181–202.

277. Chouraqui, E. 1982. Recherches sur la représentation des connaissances, le système ARCHES. In *COLING-82*, 55–60.

278. Christaller, Thomas and Dieter Metzing. 1983. Parsing interactions and a multi-level parser formalism based on cascaded ATNs. In *Automatic Natural Language Parsing*, Karen Sparck-Jones and Yorick A. Wilks, (eds.) Ellis Horwood/Wiley, Chichester/New York, 46–60.

279. Chung, Hee Sung and Tosiyasu L Kunii. 1986. NARA: a two-way simultaneous interpretation system between Korean and Japanese - a methodological study. In *COLING-86*, 325–328.

280. Church, Kenneth W. 1980. On parsing strategies and closure. In *ACL Proceedings, 18th Annual Meeting*, 107–111.

281. Church, Kenneth W. and Ramesh Patil. 1982. Coping with syntactic ambiguity or how to put the block in the box on the table. *American Journal of Computational Linguistics* 8:3–4, 139–149.

282. Church, Kenneth W. 1983. Allophonic and phonotactic constraints are useful. In *IJCAI-83*, 637–638.

283. Church, Kenneth W. 1983. A finite-state parser for use in speech recognition. In *ACL Proceedings, 21st Annual Meeting*, 91–97.

284. Church, Kenneth W. 1985. Stress assignment in letter to sound rules for speech synthesis. In *ACL Proceedings, 23rd Annual Meeting*, 246–253.

285. Church, Kenneth W. 1986. Morphological decomposition and stress assignment for speech synthesis. In *ACL Proceedings, 24th Annual Meeting*, 156–164.

286. Chytil, Michael P. and Hans Karlgren. 1986. Categorial grammars for strata on non-CF languages and their parsers. In *COLING-86*, 208–210.

287. Clark, Herbert H. and Catherine R Marshall. 1981. Definite reference and mutual knowledge. In *Elements of Discourse Understanding*, Aravind K. Joshi, Bonnie Lynn Webber and Ivan Sag, (eds.) Cambridge University Press, Cambridge, 10–62.

288. Clemente-Salazar, Marco A. 1984. Uses of C-graphs in a prototype for automatic translation. In *COLING-84*, 61–64.

289. Clifford, James. 1983. QE-III: a formal approach to natural language querying. In *AAAI-83*, 79–83.

290. Clippinger, John H., Jr. and David D McDonald. 1983. Why good writing is easier to understand. In *IJCAI-83*, 730–732.

291. Coelho, Helder. 1982. A formalism for the structural analysis of dialogues. In *COLING-82*, 61–69.

292. Coelho, Helder. 1982. Man-machine communication in Portugese: a friendly library system. *Information Systems* 2:7.

293. Cohen, Philip R. and C. Raymond Perrault. 1986 (1979). Elements of a plan-based theory of speech acts. In *Readings in Natural Language Processing*, Barbara J. Grosz, Karen Sparck-Jones and Bonnie Lynn Webber, (eds.) Morgan Kaufmann, Los Altos, 423–440.

294. Cohen, Philip R. 1980. Signalling the interpretation of indirect speech acts. In *ACL Proceedings, 18th Annual Meeting*, 29–30.

295. Cohen, Philip R. and Hector J Levesque. 1980. Speech acts and the recognition of shared plans. In *Proceedings of the Third Biennial Conference of the Canadian Society for Computational Studies of Intelligence (3rd Canadian Conference on AI)*, 263–271.

296. Cohen, Philip R. 1981. Investigation of processing strategies for the structural analysis of arguments. In *ACL Proceedings, 19th Annual Meeting*, 71–75.

297. Cohen, Philip R. 1981. The need for referent identification as a planned action. *IJCAI-81* 1, 31–36.

298. Cohen, Philip R. and C. Raymond Perrault. 1981. Elements of a plan-based theory of speech acts. In *Readings in Artificial Intelligence*, Bonnie Lynn Webber and Nils J. Nilsson, (eds.) Tioga, Palo Alto, 478–495.

299. Cohen, Philip R., Scott Fertig and Kathy Starr. 1982. Dependencies of discourse structure on the modality of communication: telephone vs. teletype. In *ACL Proceedings, 20th Annual Meeting*, 28–35.

300. Cohen, Philip R., C. Raymond Perrault and James F Allen. 1982. Beyond question answering. In *Strategies for Natural Language Processing*, Wendy G. Lehnert and Martin H. Ringle, (eds.) Erlbaum, Hillsdale, 245–274.

301. Cohen, Philip R. 1984. Referring as requesting. In *COLING-84*, 207–211.

302. Cohen, Philip R. 1984. The pragmatics of referring and the modality of communication. *Computational Linguistics* 10:2, 97–146.

303. Cohen, Philip R. and Hector J Levesque. 1985. Speech acts and rationality. In *ACL Proceedings, 23rd Annual Meeting*, 49–60.

304. Cohen, Robin. 1980. Understanding arguments. In *Proceedings of the Third Biennial Conference of the Canadian Society for Computational Studies of Intelligence (3rd Canadian Conference on AI)*, 272–279.

305. Cohen, Robin. 1984. A computational theory of the function of clue words in argument understanding. In *COLING-84*, 251–258.

306. Cohen, Robin. 1985. The need for pragmatics in natural language understanding. In *Theoretical Approaches to Natural Language Understanding, a Workshop at Halifax, Nova Scotia*, 70–77.

307. Cohen, Robin. 1987. Analyzing the structure of argumentative discourse. *Computational Linguistics* 13:1–2, 11–24.

308. Cohen, Robin. 1987. Interpreting clues in conjunction with processing restrictions in arguments and discourse. In *AAAI-87*, 528–533.

309. Colby, Kenneth M., Daniel Christinaz, Santiago Graham and Roger C Parkinson. 1980. A word finding algorithm with a dynamic lexical-semantic memory for patients with anomia using a speech prosthesis. In *AAAI-80*, 289–291.

310. Colmerauer, Alain. 1982. An interesting subset of natural language. In *Logic Programming*, Keith L. Clark and Sten-Ake Tarnlund, (eds.) Academic Press, London, 45–66.

311. Colmerauer, Alain. 1985. Nothing more than PROLOG. In *Proceedings of an International Workshop on Natural Language Understanding and Logic Programming, University of Rennes*.

312. Comino, R., R. Gemello, Giovanni Guida, C. Rullent, L. Sisto and M Somalvico. 1983. Understanding natural language through parallel processing of syntactic and semantic knowledge: an application to data base query. In *IJCAI-83*, 663–667.

313. Conklin, E. Jeffrey and David D McDonald. 1982. Salience: the key to the selection problem in natural language generation. In *ACL Proceedings, 20th Annual Meeting*, 129–135.

314. Cook, Malcom E., Wendy G. Lehnert and David D McDonald. 1984. Conveying implicit content in narrative summaries. In *COLING-84*, 5–7.

315. Cooper, Robin. 1985. Meaning representation in Montague grammar and situation semantics. In *Theoretical Approaches to Natural Language Understanding, a Workshop at Halifax, Nova Scotia*, 11.

316. Cooper, Robin. 1987. Meaning representation in Montague Grammar and situation semantics. In *Proceedings of the Alvey Sponsored Workshop on Formal Semantics in Natural Language Processing*, Barry G.T. Lowden, (ed.) University of Essex, Colchester, 24–72.

317. Cordier, M.O. and C Moghrabi. 1982. An experiment towards more efficient automatic translation. In *ECAI-82*, 228–231.

318. Correa, Nelson. 1987. An attribute-grammar implementation of government-binding theory. In *ACL Proceedings, 25th Annual Meeting*, 45–51.

319. Correira, Alfred. 1980. Computing story trees. *American Journal of Computational Linguistics* 6:3–4, 135–149.

320. Cottrell, Garrison W. and Steven L Small. 1984. Viewing parsing as word sense discrimination. In *Computational Models of Natural Language Processing*, Bruno G. Bara and Giovanni Guida, (eds.) North-Holland, Amsterdam, 91–119.

321. Cottrell, Garrison W. 1987. Toward connectionist semantics. In *TINLAP-3*, 63–67.

322. Courant, Michèle and Sophie Robin. 1985. Classified advertisement analysis in the context of an expert system in AD matching. In *Natural Language Understanding and Logic Programming*, Veronica Dahl and Patrick Saint-Dizier, (eds.) North-Holland, Amsterdam, 33–47.

323. Covington, Alan R. and Lenhart K Schubert. 1980. Organization of modally embedded propositions and of dependent concepts. In *Proceedings of the Third Biennial Conference of the Canadian Society for Computational Studies of Intelligence (3rd Canadian Conference on AI)*, 87–94.

324. Cowie, James R. 1983. Automatic analysis of descriptive texts. In *ACL Proceedings, Conference on Applied Natural Language Processing*, 117–123.

325. Crain, Stephen and Janet D Fodor. 1985. How can grammars help parsers?. In *Natural Language Parsing*, David R. Dowty, Lauri Karttunen and Arnold M. Zwicky, (eds.) Cambridge University Press, Cambridge, 94–128.

326. Crain, Stephen and Mark J Steedman. 1985. On not being led up the garden path: the use of context by the psychological syntax processor. In *Natural Language Parsing*, David R. Dowty, Lauri Karttunen and Arnold M. Zwicky, (eds.) Cambridge University Press, Cambridge, 320–358.

327. Critz, J.T. 1982. Frame based recognition of theme continuity. In *COLING-82*, 71–75.

328. Crout, J. Norwood. 1981. Untitled. In *ACL Proceedings, 19th Annual Meeting*, 31–32.

329. Cudazzo, Raffaele, Leonardo Lesmo and Claudia Randi. 1984. Interpretation of natural language queries via pattern-action rules. In *Artificial Intelligence and Information-Control Systems of Robots*, Ivan Plander, (ed.) North-Holland, Amsterdam, 119–122.

330. Cullingford, Richard E. 1986 (1981). SAM. In *Readings in Natural Language Processing*, Barbara J. Grosz, Karen Sparck-Jones and Bonnie Lynn Webber, (eds.) Morgan Kaufmann, Los Altos, 627–649.

331. Cullingford, Richard E. 1981. SAM. In *Inside Computer Understanding: Five Programs plus Miniatures*, Roger C. Schank and Christopher K. Riesbeck, (eds.) Erlbaum, Hillsdale, 75–119.

332. Cullingford, Richard E. 1981. Micro SAM. In *Inside Computer Understanding: Five Programs plus Miniatures*, Roger C. Schank and Christopher K. Riesbeck, (eds.) Erlbaum, Hillsdale, 120–135.

333. Cullingford, Richard E., M.W. Krueger, Mallory Selfridge and M.A Bienkowski. 1981. Towards automating explanations. *IJCAI-81* 1, 362–367.

334. Cullingford, Richard E. 1985. *Natural Language Processing: a Knowledge Engineering Approach*. Rowan & Allanheld, Totowa.

335. Cullingford, Richard E. and Boyan A Onyshkevych. 1987. An experiment in lexicon driven machine translation. In *Machine Translation: Theoretical and Methodological Issues*, Sergei Nirenberg, (ed.) Cambridge University Press, Cambridge, 278–301.

336. Cushing, Steven. 1983. Abstract control structures and the semantics of quantifiers. In *ACL Proceedings, First European Conference*, 1–8.

337. Cyre, Walling. 1985. The design of a restricted sublanguage. In *Theoretical Approaches to Natural Language Understanding, a Workshop at Halifax, Nova Scotia*, 128–130.

338. Dahl, Deborah, Martha Palmer and Rebecca Passoneau. 1987. Nominalizations in PUNDIT. In *ACL Proceedings, 25th Annual Meeting*, 131–139.

339. Dahl, Deborah A. 1986. Focusing and and reference resolution in PUNDIT. *AAAI-86* 2, 1083–1088.

340. Dahl, Deborah A. 1987. Determiners, entities, and contexts. In *TINLAP-3*, 133–136.

341. Dahl, Osten. 1986. The interpretation of bound pronouns. In *Papers from the Fifth Scandinavian Conference of Computational Linguistics*, Fred Karlsson, (ed.) University of Helsinki, Helsinki, 49–58.

342. Dahl, Veronica. 1980. A three-valued logic for natural language question-answering systems. In *Proceedings of the 10th International Symposium on Multiple-Valued Logic*.

343. Dahl, Veronica. 1981. Translating Spanish into logic through logic. *American Journal of Computational Linguistics* 7:3, 149–164.

344. Dahl, Veronica. 1983. Current trends in logic grammars. In *Workshop on logic programming, Algarve, Portugal*.

345. Dahl, Veronica and Michael C McCord. 1983. Treating coordination in logic grammars. *American Journal of Computational Linguistics* 9:2, 69–91.

346. Dahl, Veronica. 1984. More on gapping grammars. In *Proceedings of the International Conference on Fifth Generation Computer Systems*, ICOT, Tokyo, 669–677.

347. Dahl, Veronica and Harvey Abramson. 1984. On gapping grammars. In *Proceedings of the Second International Logic Programming Conference, Uppsala, Sweden*, 77–88.

348. Dahl, Veronica. 1985. Hiding complexity from the casual writer of parsers. In *Natural Language Understanding and Logic Programming*, Veronica Dahl and Patrick Saint-Dizier, (eds.) North-Holland, Amsterdam, 1–19.

349. Dahl, Veronica and Patrick Saint-Dizier, (eds.) 1985. *Natural Language Understanding and Logic Programming*. North-Holland, Amsterdam.

350. Dahlgreen, Kathleen and J McDowell. 1986. Kind types in knowledge representation. In *COLING-86*, 216–221.

351. Dahlgreen, Kathleen and J McDowell. 1986. Using commonsense knowledge to disambiguate prepositional phrase modifiers. *AAAI-86* 1, 589–593.

352. Dailey, David P. 1986. The extraction of a minimum set of semantic primitives from a monolingual dictionary is NP-complete. *Computational Linguistics* 12:4, 306–307.

353. Daladier, Anne. 1985. Programming in a natural language - at what cost?. In *Natural Language Understanding and Logic Programming*, Veronica Dahl and Patrick Saint-Dizier, (eds.) North-Holland, Amsterdam, 221–232.

354. Damerau, Fred J. 1981. Operating statistics for the transformational question answering system. *American Journal of Computational Linguistics* 7:1, 30–42.

355. Danlos, Laurence. 1983. Some issues in generation from a semantic representation. In *IJCAI-83*, 606–609.

356. Danlos, Laurence. 1984. Conceptual and linguistic decisions in generation. In *COLING-84*, 501–504.

357. Danlos, Laurence. 1984. An algorithm for automatic generation. In *ECAI-84*, 213–215.

358. Danlos, Laurence, Eric Laporte and Francoise Emerard. 1986. Synthesis of spoken messages from semantic representations (semantic-representation-to-speech-system). In *COLING-86*, 599–604.

359. Danlos, Laurence. 1987. *The Linguistic Basis of Text Generation.* Cambridge University Press, Cambridge.

360. Davidson, James and S. Jerrold Kaplan. 1980. Parsing in the absence of a complete lexicon. In *ACL Proceedings, 18th Annual Meeting*, 105–106.

361. Davidson, James and S. Jerrold Kaplan. 1983. Natural language access to data bases: interpreting update requests. *American Journal of Computational Linguistics* 9:2, 57–68.

362. Davison, Alice and Richard Lutz. 1985. Measuring syntactic complexity relative to discourse context. In *Natural Language Parsing*, David R. Dowty, Lauri Karttunen and Arnold M. Zwicky, (eds.) Cambridge University Press, Cambridge, 26–66.

363. Debili, Fathi. 1982. A method of automatic word family building. In *Deontic Logic, Computational Linguistics and Legal Information Systems*, Antonio A. Martino, (ed.) North-Holland, Amsterdam, 305–325.

364. Decker, Nan. 1985. The use of syntactic clues in discourse processing. In *ACL Proceedings, 23rd Annual Meeting*, 315–323.

365. Dehn, Natalie. 1981. Story generation after TALE-SPIN. *IJCAI-81* 1, 16–18.

366. DeJong, Gerald F. 1981. Generalizations based on explanations. *IJCAI-81* 1, 67–69.

367. DeJong, Gerald F. 1982. An overview of the FRUMP system. In *Strategies for Natural Language Processing*, Wendy G. Lehnert and Martin H. Ringle, (eds.) Erlbaum, Hillsdale, 149–176.

368. DeJong, Gerald F. and David L Waltz. 1983. Understanding novel language. *Computers and Mathematics with Applications* 9:1, 131–147.

369. Dell, Gary S. 1984. Positive feedback in hierarchical connectionist models: applications to language production. *Cognitive Science* 9:1, 3–24.

370. Delmonte, Rodolfo. 1983. A phonological processor for Italian. In *ACL Proceedings, First European Conference*, 26–34.

371. Delmonte, Rodolfo. 1985. Parsing difficulties and phonological processing in Italian. In *ACL Proceedings, Second European Conference*, 136–145.

372. Del Cerro, Luis Farinas and Said Soulhi. 1985. Mutual belief logic for processing definite reference. In *Natural Language Understanding and Logic Programming*, Veronica Dahl and Patrick Saint-Dizier, (eds.) North-Holland, Amsterdam, 65–78.

373. Del Cerro, Luis Farinas and Said Soulhi. 1985. Mutual belief logic for processing definite reference. In *Proceedings of an International Workshop on Natural Language Understanding and Logic Programming, University of Rennes*.

374. Derr, Marcia A. and Kathleen R McKeown. 1984. Using focus to generate complex and simple sentences. In *COLING-84*, 319–326.

375. Devadason, F.J. 1980. Generation of thesaurus in different languages: a computer based system. In *COLING-80*, 303–314.

376. Dey, Pradip. 1986. Processing word order variation within a modified ID/LP framework. In *COLING-86*, 65–67.

377. De Mori, Renato, Attilio Giordano, Lorenza Saitta and Pietro Laface. 1982. An expert system for interpreting speech patterns. In *AAAI-82*, 107–110.

378. De Mori, Renato and Mathew Palakal. 1985. On the use of a taxonomy of time-frequency. *IJCAI-85* 2, 877–879.

379. De Roeck, Anne N. 1983. An underview of parsing. In *Parsing Natural Language*, Margaret King, (ed.) Academic Press, London, 3–17.

380. De Roeck, Anne N. and Barry G.T Lowden. 1986. Generating English paraphrases from formal relational calculus expressions. In *COLING-86*, 581–583.

381. De Smedt, Koenraad. 1984. Using object-oriented knowledge-representation techniques in morphology and syntax programming. In *ECAI-84*, 181–184.

382. Dilger, Werner. 1980. Automatic translation with attribute grammars. In *COLING-80*, 397–404.

383. Dilger, Werner. 1982. Tree directed grammars. In *COLING-82*, 77–82.

384. Dinenberg, F.G. 1986. Communicative triad as a structural element of language interaction. In *COLING-86*, 232–234.

385. Di Eigenio, Barbara, Leonardo Lesmo, Paolo Pogliano, Pietro Torasso and Francesco Urbano. 1986. A logical formalism for the representation of determiners. In *COLING-86*, 344–346.

386. Dogil, Grzegorz. 1986. Phonological pivot parsing. In *COLING-86*, 615–617.

387. Domenig, Marc and Patrick Shann. 1986. Towards a dedicated database management system for dictionaries. In *COLING-86*, 91–96.

388. Dorr, Bonnie. 1987. UNITRAN: an interlingual approach to machine translation. In *AAAI-87*, 534–539.

389. Dowty, David R., Lauri Karttunen and Arnold M. Zwicky, (eds.) 1985. *Natural Language Parsing*. Cambridge University Press, Cambridge.

390. Dreizin, F., A. Shenhar and H Bar-Itzhak. 1980. A formal grammar of expressiveness for sacred legends. In *COLING-80*, 159–166.

391. Duffy, Gavan and John C Mallery. 1984. Referential determinism and computational efficiency: posting constraints from deep structure. In *AAAI-84*, 101–105.

392. Duffy, Gavan. 1986. Categorical disambiguation. *AAAI-86* 2, 1079–1082.

393. Dunin-Keplicz, Barbara. 1983. Towards better understanding of anaphora. In *ACL Proceedings, First European Conference*, 139–143.

394. Dunin-Keplicz, Barbara. 1984. Default reasoning in anaphora resolution. In *ECAI-84*, 157–166.

395. Dunin-Keplicz, Barbara. 1985. How to restrict ambiguity of discourse. In *ACL Proceedings, Second European Conference*, 93–97.

396. Dunin-Keplicz, Barbara. 1985. Default reasoning in anaphora resolution. In *Advances in Artificial Intelligence*, Tim O'Shea, (ed.) North-Holland, Amsterdam, 315–324.

397. Dunin-Keplicz, Barbara and Witold Lukaszewicz. 1986. Towards discourse-oriented nonmonotonic system. In *COLING-86*, 504–506.

398. Dyer, Michael G., Thomas C. Wolf and Martin Korsin. 1981. BORIS - an in-depth understander of narratives. *IJCAI-81* 2, 1057.

399. Dyer, Michael G. 1981. Integration, unification, reconstruction, modification: an eternal parsing braid. *IJCAI-81* 1, 37–42.

400. Dyer, Michael G. 1982. Affect processing for narratives. In *AAAI-82*, 265–268.

401. Dyer, Michael G. and Uri Zernik. 1986. Encoding and acquiring meanings for figurative phrases. In *ACL Proceedings, 24th Annual Meeting*, 106–111.

402. Dyer, Michael G. 1986. *In-Depth Understanding: A Computer Model of Integrated Processing for Narrative Comprehension*. MIT Press, Cambridge, Massachusetts.

403. Dyer, Michael G., Margot Flowers and Jack Hodges. 1987. Naive mechanics comprehension and invention in EDISON. *IJCAI-87* 2, 696–699.

404. Dymetman, Marc. 1986. Two approaches to commonsense inferencing for discourse analysis. In *COLING-86*, 511–514.

405. Earley, Jay. 1986 (1970). An efficient context-free parsing algorithm. In *Readings in Natural Language Processing*, Barbara J. Grosz, Karen Sparck-Jones and Bonnie Lynn Webber, (eds.) Morgan Kaufmann, Los Altos, 25–33.

406. Ehrlich, Kate. 1981. Search and inference strategies in pronoun resolution: an experimental study. In *ACL Proceedings, 19th Annual Meeting*, 89–93.

407. Eisele, Andreas and Jochen Dörre. 1986. A lexical functional grammar system in PROLOG. In *COLING-86*, 551–553.

408. Eiselt, Kurt. 1987. Recovering from erroneous inferences. In *AAAI-87*, 540–544.

409. Eiselt, Kurt P. 1985. A parallel-process model of on-line inference processing. *IJCAI-85* 2, 863–869.

410. Ejerhed, Eva. 1982. The processing of unbounded dependencies in Swedish. In *Readings on Unbounded Dependencies in Scandinavian Languages*, Elisabet Engdahl and Eva Ejerhed, (eds.) Almqvist & Wiksell, Stockholm, 99–149.

411. Ejerhed, Eva and Hank Bromley. 1986. A self-extending lexicon: description of a word learning program. In *Papers from the Fifth Scandinavian Conference of Computational Linguistics*, Fred Karlsson, (ed.) University of Helsinki, Helsinki, 59–72.

412. Elia, Annibale and Yvette Mathieu. 1986. Computational comparative studies on romance languages. In *COLING-86*, 146–150.

413. Ellman, Jeremy. 1983. An indirect Approach to types of speech acts. In *IJCAI-83*, 600–602.

414. Elmi, Giancarlo Taddei. 1982. Logic, linguistics and legal thesauri. In *Deontic Logic, Computational Linguistics and Legal Information Systems*, Antonio A. Martino, (ed.) North-Holland, Amsterdam, 291–303.

415. Endo, Tsutomu and Tuneo Tamati. 1980. Decomposition of Japanese sentences into normal forms based on human linguistic process. In *COLING-80*, 492–499.

416. Engdahl, Elisabet. 1985. Interpreting questions. In *Natural Language Parsing*, David R. Dowty, Lauri Karttunen and Arnold M. Zwicky, (eds.) Cambridge University Press, Cambridge, 67–93.

417. Enomoto, Hajime, Naoki Yonezaki, Motoshi Saeki, Kazuhiko Chiba, Takashi Takizuka and Toshio Yokoi. 1984. Natural language based software development system TELL. In *ECAI-84*, 721–731.

418. Enomoto, Hajime, Naoki Yonezaki, Motoshi Saeki and Hiroshi Aramata. 1984. Formal specification and verification for concurrent systems by TELL. In *ECAI-84*, 732–745.

419. Erman, Lee D., Frederick Hayes-Roth, Victor R. Lesser and D. Raj Reddy. 1981. The Hearsay-II speech-understanding system: integrating knowledge to resolve uncertainty. In *Readings in Artificial Intelligence*, Bonnie Lynn Webber and Nils J. Nilsson, (eds.) Tioga, Palo Alto, 349–389.

420. Eugenio, Barbara Di and Leonardo Lesmo. 1987. Representation and interpretation of determiners in natural language. *IJCAI-87* 2, 648–654.

421. Euzenat, Bernard, Bernard Normier, Antione Ogonowski and Gian Piero Zarri. 1985. SAPHIR+RESEDA: a new approach to intelligent data base access. *IJCAI-85* 2, 855–857.

422. Evans, David A. 1981. A situation semantics approach to the analysis of speech acts. In *ACL Proceedings, 19th Annual Meeting*, 113–116.

423. Evans, Roger. 1985. ProGram - a development tool for GPSG grammars. *Linguistics* 23:2, 213–243.

424. Evans, Roger. 1987. Direct interpretations of the GPSG formalism. In *Advances in Artificial Intelligence (Proceedings of AISB-87)*, Christopher S. Mellish and John Hallam, (eds.) Wiley, Chichester, 183–193.

425. Evens, Martha, James Vandendorpe and Yih-Chen Wang. 1985. Lexical-semantic relations for information retrieval. In *Humans and Machines: 4th Delaware Symposium on Language Studies*, Stephanie Williams, (ed.) Ablex, Norwood, 73–101.

426. Fass, Dan and Yorick A Wilks. 1983. Preference semantics, ill-formedness, and metaphor. *American Journal of Computational Linguistics* 9:3–4, 178–187.

427. Fass, Dan. 1986. Collative semantics. In *COLING-86*, 341–343.

428. Fawcett, Brenda and Graeme Hirst. 1986. The detection and representation of ambiguities of intension and description. In *ACL Proceedings, 24th Annual Meeting*, 192–199.

429. Fábricz, Károly. 1986. Particle homonymy and machine translation. In *COLING-86*, 59–61.

430. Ferber, Jacques. 1984. MERING: an open-ended object oriented language for knowledge representation. In *ECAI-84*, 195–204.

431. Ferrari, Giacomo and Oliviero Stock. 1980. Strategy selection for an ATN syntactic parser. In *ACL Proceedings, 18th Annual Meeting*, 113–115.

432. Ferrari, Giacomo and Ronan Reilly. 1986. A two-level dialogue representation. In *COLING-86*, 42–45.

433. Filgueiras, M. 1983. A kernel for a general natural language interface. In *Workshop on logic programming, Algarve, Portugal*.

434. Fimbel, E., H. Groscot, Jean-Marie Lancel and Nathalie Simonin. 1985. Using a text model for analysis and generation. In *ACL Proceedings, Second European Conference*, 226–231.

435. Finin, Timothy W. 1980. The semantic interpretation of nominal compounds. In *AAAI-80*, 310–312.

436. Finin, Timothy W. and Martha S Palmer. 1983. Parsing with logical variables. In *ACL Proceedings, Conference on Applied Natural Language Processing*, 62–68.

437. Flickinger, Daniel P. 1984. Panel on natural language and databases. In *COLING-84*, 188–189.

438. Flickinger, Daniel P. 1985. Using the head in natural language processing. In *Theoretical Approaches to Natural Language Understanding, a Workshop at Halifax, Nova Scotia*, 12.

439. Flickinger, Daniel P., Carl J. Pollard and Thomas Wasow. 1985. Structure-sharing in lexical representation. In *ACL Proceedings, 23rd Annual Meeting*, 262–267.

440. Flowers, Margot, Rod McGuire and Lawrence Birnbaum. 1982. Adversary arguments and the logic of personal attacks. In *Strategies for Natural Language Processing*, Wendy G. Lehnert and Martin H. Ringle, (eds.) Erlbaum, Hillsdale, 275–297.

441. Flowers, Margot. 1982. On being contradictory. In *AAAI-82*, 269–272.

442. Fodor, Janet D. 1980. Is the human sentence parsing mechanism an ATN?. *Cognition* 8, 417–459.

443. Fong, Sandiway and Robert C Berwick. 1985. New approaches to parsing conjunctions using PROLOG. *IJCAI-85* 2, 870–876.

444. Fornell, Jan. 1984. What not to say. In *COLING-84*, 348–351.

445. Frazier, Lyn. 1985. Syntactic complexity. In *Natural Language Parsing*, David R. Dowty, Lauri Karttunen and Arnold M. Zwicky, (eds.) Cambridge University Press, Cambridge, 129–189.

446. Frederking, Robert E. 1981. A rule-based conversation participant. In *ACL Proceedings, 19th Annual Meeting*, 83–86.

447. Frey, Werner and Uwe Reyle. 1983. A PROLOG implementation of lexical functional grammar as a base for a natural language processing system. In *ACL Proceedings, First European Conference*, 52–57.

448. Frey, Werner, Uwe Reyle and Christian Rohrer. 1983. Analysing texts in natural language. In *IJCAI-83*, 727–729.

449. Frey, Werner. 1985. Noun phrases in lexical functional grammar. In *Natural Language Understanding and Logic Programming*, Veronica Dahl and Patrick Saint-Dizier, (eds.) North-Holland, Amsterdam, 121–137.

450. Friedman, Joyce, Dawei Dai and Weiguo Wang. 1986. The weak generative capacity of parenthesis-free categorial grammars. In *COLING-86*, 199–201.

451. Friedman, Joyce and Ramarathnam Venkatesan. 1986. Categorial and non-categorial languages. In *ACL Proceedings, 24th Annual Meeting*, 75–77.

452. Frisch, Alan M. and Donald Perlis. 1981. A re-evaluation of story grammars. *Cognitive Science* 5:1, 79–86.

453. Frisch, Alan M. 1985. Parsing with restricted quantification. In *AISB-85*, 196–208.

454. Frisch, Alan M. 1986. Parsing with restricted quantification: an initial demonstration. *Computational Intelligence* 2:3, 142–150.

455. Frost, David P. 1987. A natural language interface for expert systems: system architecture. In *Advances in Artificial Intelligence (Proceedings of AISB-87)*, Christopher S. Mellish and John Hallam, (eds.) Wiley, Chichester, 157–168.

456. Fujisaki, Tetsunosuke. 1984. A stochastic approach to sentence parsing. In *COLING-84*, 16–19.

457. Fum, Danilo, Giovanni Guida and Carlo Tasso. 1982. Forward and backward reasoning in automatic abstracting. In *COLING-82*, 83–88.

458. Fum, Danilo, Giovanni Guida and Carlo Tasso. 1984. A propositional language for text representation. In *Computational Models of Natural Language Processing*, Bruno G. Bara and Giovanni Guida, (eds.) North-Holland, Amsterdam, 121–150.

459. Fum, Danilo. 1984. Inferential reasoning in natural language processing. In *Artificial Intelligence and Information-Control Systems of Robots*, Ivan Plander, (ed.) North-Holland, Amsterdam, 139–142.

460. Fum, Danilo. 1985. Natural language processing and the automatic acquisition of knowledge: a simulative approach. In *ACL Proceedings, Second European Conference*, 79–88.

461. Fum, Danilo, Giovanni Guida and Carlo Tasso. 1985. A rule-based approach to evaluating importance in descriptive texts. In *ACL Proceedings, Second European Conference*, 244–250.

462. Fum, Danilo, Giovanni Guida and Carlo Tasso. 1985. Evaluating importance: a step towards text summarisation. *IJCAI-85* 2, 840–844.

463. Fum, Danilo, Giovanni Guida and Carlo Tasso. 1986. Tailoring importance evaluation to reader's goals: a contribution to descriptive text summarization. In *COLING-86*, 256–259.

464. Furugori, Teiji. 1981. Computing a map from michi-annai-bun or written descriptions. *IJCAI-81* 1, 426–428.

465. Garnham, Alan, Jane Oakhill and Philip N Johnson-Laird. 1982. Referential continuity and the coherence of discourse. *Cognition* 11, 29–46.

466. Garnham, Alan. 1983. What's wrong with story grammars?. *Cognition* 15, 145–154.

467. Garside, Roger and Fanny Leech. 1985. A probabilistic parser. In *ACL Proceedings, Second European Conference*, 166–170.

468. Gawron, Jean M., Jonathan King, John Lamping, Egon Loebner, E. Anne Paulson, Geoffrey K. Pullum, Ivan A. Sag and Thomas Wasow. 1982. Processing English with a generalized phrase structure grammar. In *ACL Proceedings, 20th Annual Meeting*, 74–81.

469. Gayek, Oliver, Hanno T. Beck, Diane Elder and Greg Whittemore. 1983. Lisp implementation. *Texas Linguistic Forum* 22, 187–202.

470. Gazdar, Gerald. 1981. Speech act assignment. In *Elements of Discourse Understanding*, Aravind K. Joshi, Bonnie Lynn Webber and Ivan Sag, (eds.) Cambridge University Press, Cambridge, 63–83.

471. Gazdar, Gerald. 1983. Phrase structure grammars and natural languages. In *IJCAI-83*, 556–565.

472. Gazdar, Gerald. 1983. NLs, CFLs and CF-PSGs. In *Automatic Natural Language Parsing*, Karen Sparck-Jones and Yorick A. Wilks, (eds.) Ellis Horwood/Wiley, Chichester/New York, 81–93.

473. Gazdar, Gerald. 1984. Recent computer implementations of PSGs. *Computational Linguistics* 10:3–4, 212–214.

474. Gazdar, Gerald. 1985. Review article: finite state morphology. *Linguistics* 23:4, 597–607.

475. Gazdar, Gerald. 1985. Computational tools for doing linguistics: introduction. *Linguistics* 23:2, 185–187.

476. Gazdar, Gerald. 1985. Linguistic applications of default inheritance mechanisms. In *Proceedings of the Alvey/ICL Workshop on Linguistic Theory and Computer Applications*, Peter Whitelock, Harold Somers, Paul Bennett, Rod L. Johnson and Mary McGee Wood, (eds.) CCL/UMIST, Manchester, 27–48.

477. Gazdar, Gerald and Geoffrey K Pullum. 1985. Computationally relevant properties of natural languages and their grammars. *New Generation Computing* 3, 273–306.

478. Gazdar, Gerald. 1987. COMIT ==>* PATR II. In *TINLAP-3*, 37–39.

479. Gehrke, Manfred. 1983. A multilevel approach to handle non-standard input. In *ACL Proceedings, First European Conference*, 183–187.

480. Gehrke, Manfred. 1983. Syntax, semantics, and pragmatics in concert: an incremental, multilevel approach in reconstructing task-oriented dialogues. In *IJCAI-83*, 721–723.

481. Gentner, Dedre, Brian Falkenhainer and Janice Skorstad. 1987. Metaphor: the good, the bad and the ugly. In *TINLAP-3*, 155–159.

482. Gershman, Anatole V. 1981. Figuring out what the user wants: steps toward an automatic yellow pages assistant. *IJCAI-81* 1, 423–425.

483. Gershman, Anatole V. 1982. A framework for conceptual analyzers. In *Strategies for Natural Language Processing*, Wendy G. Lehnert and Martin H. Ringle, (eds.) Erlbaum, Hillsdale, 177–201.

484. Gigley, Helen M. 1984. From HOPE en L'ESPERANCE: on the role of computational neurolinguistics in cross language studies. In *COLING-84*, 452–456.

485. Gigley, Helen M. 1985. Computational neurolinguistics - what is it all about?. *IJCAI-85* 1, 260–266.

486. Gigley, Helen M. 1985. Grammar viewed as a functioning part of a cognitive system. In *ACL Proceedings, 23rd Annual Meeting*, 324–332.

487. Gillott, Timothy J. 1985. The simulation of stress patterns in synthetic speech - a two-level problem. In *ACL Proceedings, Second European Conference*, 232–238.

488. Ginsparg, Jerrold M. 1983. A robust portable natural language data base interface. In *ACL Proceedings, Conference on Applied Natural Language Processing*, 25–30.

489. Glasgow III, John C. 1987. YANLI: a powerful natural language front-end tool. *The AI Magazine* 8:1, 40–48.

490. Goerz, Guenther. 1980. The HEX-system: Experiences with an expectation-based parser. In *Natural Language Based Computer Systems*, Leonard Bolc, (ed.) Hanser, Munich, 319–354.

491. Goerz, Guenther. 1981. GLP: a general linguistic processor. *IJCAI-81* 1, 429–431.

492. Goerz, Guenther. 1982. Applying a chart parser to speech understanding. In *ECAI-82*, 257–258.

493. Goerz, Guenther and C Beckstein. 1983. How to parse gaps in spoken utterances. In *ACL Proceedings, First European Conference*, 111–113.

494. Goeser, S. and E Mergenthaler. 1986. TBMS: domain specific text management and lexicon development. In *COLING-86*, 235–240.

495. Golding, Andrew R. and Henry S Thompson. 1985. A morphology component for language programs. *Linguistics* 23:2, 263–284.

496. Gomez, Fernando. 1982. Towards a theory of comprehension of declarative contexts. In *ACL Proceedings, 20th Annual Meeting*, 36–43.

497. Gomez, Fernando. 1985. A model of comprehension of elementary scientific texts. In *Theoretical Approaches to Natural Language Understanding, a Workshop at Halifax, Nova Scotia*, 78–88.

498. Goodman, Bradley A. 1983. Repairing miscommunication: relaxation in reference. In *AAAI-83*, 134–138.

499. Goodman, Bradley A. 1985. Repairing reference identification failures by relaxation. In *ACL Proceedings, 23rd Annual Meeting*, 204–217.

500. Goodman, Bradley A. 1986. Reference identification and reference identification failures. *Computational Linguistics* 12:4, 273–305.

501. Goodman, Bradley A. 1987. Reference and reference failures. In *TINLAP-3*, 150–154.

502. Granacki, John J., Alice C. Parker and Yigal Arens. 1987. Understanding system specifications written in natural language. *IJCAI-87* 2, 688–691.

503. Grandjean, Ernest and Gerard Veillon. 1980. Une experience pratique d'utilisation de l'analyse linguistique en recherche d'information: bilan & perspectives. In *COLING-80*, 512–513.

504. Granger, Richard H. 1980. When expectation fails: towards a self-correcting inference system. In *AAAI-80*, 301–305.

505. Granger, Richard H. 1981. Directing and redirecting inference pursuit: extra-textual influences on text interpretation. *IJCAI-81* 1, 354–361.

506. Granger, Richard H. 1982. Scruffy text understanding: design and implementation of 'tolerant' understanders. In *ACL Proceedings, 20th Annual Meeting*, 157–160.

507. Granger, Richard H. 1983. The NOMAD system: expectation-based detection and correction of errors during understanding of syntactically and semantically ill-formed text. *American Journal of Computational Linguistics* 9:3–4, 188–196.

508. Granger, Richard H., Chris J. Staros, Gregory B. Taylor and Rika Yoshii. 1983. Scruffy text understanding: design and implementation of the NOMAD system. In *ACL Proceedings, Conference on Applied Natural Language Processing*, 104–106.

509. Granville, Robert. 1984. Controlling lexical substitution in computer text generation. In *COLING-84*, 381–384.

510. Grau, Brigitte. 1984. Stalking 'coherence' in the topical jungle. In *Proceedings of the International Conference on Fifth Generation Computer Systems*, ICOT, Tokyo, 652–659.

511. Green, Bert F., Alice K. Wolf, Carol Chomsky and Kenneth Laughery. 1986 (1961). BASEBALL: an automatic question answerer. In *Readings in Natural Language Processing*, Barbara J. Grosz, Karen Sparck-Jones and Bonnie Lynn Webber, (eds.) Morgan Kaufmann, Los Altos, 545–549.

512. Grimes, Joseph E. 1980. System support in Chinese data entry. In *COLING-80*, 283–286.

513. Grimes, Joseph E. 1984. Denormalisation and cross referencing in theoretical lexicography. In *COLING-84*, 38–41.

514. Grishman, Ralph. 1980. Conjunctions and modularity in Language analysis procedures. In *COLING-80*, 500–503.

515. Grishman, Ralph. 1981. Parsing. In *ACL Proceedings, 19th Annual Meeting*, 101–102.

516. Grishman, Ralph, Lynette Hirschman and C Friedman. 1982. Natural language interfaces using limited semantic information. In *COLING-82*, 89–94.

517. Grishman, Ralph, Lynette Hirschman and C Friedman. 1983. Isolating domain dependencies in natural language interfaces. In *ACL Proceedings, Conference on Applied Natural Language Processing*, 46–53.

518. Grishman, Ralph and Richard Kittridge, (eds.) 1986. *Analyzing Language in Restricted Domains: Sublanguage Description and Processing*. Lawrence Erlbaum, Hillsdale, New Jersey.

519. Grishman, Ralph. 1986. *Computational Linguistics: An Introduction*. Cambridge University Press, Cambridge.

520. Grishman, Ralph, Ngo Than Nhan, Elaine Marsh and Lynette Hirschman. 1984. Automated determination of sublanguage syntactic usage. In *COLING-84*, 96–100.

521. Grishman, Ralph, Lynette Hirschman and Ngo Than Nhan. 1986. Discovery procedures for sublanguage selectional patterns: initial experiments. *Computational Linguistics* 12:3, 205–215.

522. Gross, Maurice. 1984. Lexicon-grammar and the syntactic analysis of French. In *COLING-84*, 275–282.

523. Gross, Maurice. 1986. Lexicon grammar: the representation of compound words. In *COLING-86*, 1–6.

524. Grosz, Barbara J. 1986 (1977). The representation and use of focus in a system for understanding dialogs. In *Readings in Natural Language Processing*, Barbara J. Grosz, Karen Sparck-Jones and Bonnie Lynn Webber, (eds.) Morgan Kaufmann, Los Altos, 353–362.

525. Grosz, Barbara J. 1980. Interactive discourse: influence of problem context. In *ACL Proceedings, 18th Annual Meeting*, 25.

526. Grosz, Barbara J. 1981. Focusing and description in natural language dialogues. In *Elements of Discourse Understanding*, Aravind K. Joshi, Bonnie Lynn Webber and Ivan Sag, (eds.) Cambridge University Press, Cambridge, 84–105.

527. Grosz, Barbara J., N. Haas, Gary G. Hendrix, Jerry R. Hobbs, Paul Martin, Robert C. Moore, Jane J. Robinson and Stanley J Rosenschein. 1982. DIALOGIC: a core natural-language processing system. In *COLING-82*, 95–100.

528. Grosz, Barbara J. 1982. Transportable natural-language interfaces: problems and techniques. In *ACL Proceedings, 20th Annual Meeting*, 46–50.

529. Grosz, Barbara J. 1982. Natural language processing. *Artificial Intelligence* 19:2, 131–136.

530. Grosz, Barbara J., Aravind K. Joshi and Scott Weinstein. 1983. Providing a unified account of definite noun phrases in discourse. In *ACL Proceedings, 21st Annual Meeting*, 44–50.

531. Grosz, Barbara J. 1983. TEAM, a transportable natural language interface system. In *ACL Proceedings, Conference on Applied Natural Language Processing*, 39–45.

532. Grosz, Barbara J. and Candace L Sidner. 1985. Discourse structure and the proper treatment of interruptions. *IJCAI-85* 2, 832–839.

533. Grosz, Barbara J. 1985. Natural-language processing. *Artificial Intelligence* 25:1, 1–4.

534. Grosz, Barbara J. and Candace L Sidner. 1986. Attentions, intentions, and the structure of discourse. *Computational Linguistics* 12:3, 175–204.

535. Grosz, Barbara J., Karen Sparck-Jones and Bonnie Lynn Webber, (eds.) 1986. *Readings in Natural Language Processing*. Morgan Kaufmann, Los Altos.

536. Grosz, Barbara J. 1987. Whither discourse and speech acts ?. In *TINLAP-3*, 84–85.

537. Grover, Mark D. 1982. A synthetic approach to temporal information processing. In *AAAI-82*, 91–94.

538. Guenther, Franz and Hubert Lehmann. 1983. Rules for pronominalization. In *ACL Proceedings, First European Conference*, 144–151.

539. Guenther, Franz and Hubert Lehmann. 1984. Automatic construction of discourse representation structures. In *COLING-84*, 398–401.

540. Guenthner, Franz. 1987. Panel on discourse analysis. In *TINLAP-3*, 100.

541. Guida, Giovanni. 1980. Goal oriented parsing: improving the efficiency of natural language access to relational data bases. In *COLING-80*, 550–557.

542. Guida, Giovanni and Carlo Tasso. 1983. IR-NLI: an expert natural language interface to online data bases. In *ACL Proceedings, Conference on Applied Natural Language Processing*, 31–38.

543. Guida, Giovanni and Giancarlo Mauri. 1984. A formal basis for performance evaluation of natural language understanding systems. *Computational Linguistics* 10:1, 15–30.

544. Guilbaud, Hean-Philippe. 1986. Variables et categories grammaticales dans un modele ARIANE. In *COLING-86*, 405–407.

545. Guindon, Raymonde. 1985. Anaphora resolution: short-term memory and focusing. In *ACL Proceedings, 23rd Annual Meeting*, 218–227.

546. Guindon, Raymonde. 1986. The structure of task-oriented dialogues: evidence from subdialogue boundary markers and the distribution of anaphors and their antecedents. In *ACL Proceedings, 24th Annual Meeting*, 224–230.

547. Guindon, Raymonde, Kelly Shuldberg and Joyce Connor. 1987. Grammatical and ungrammatical structures in user-adviser dialogues. In *ACL Proceedings, 25th Annual Meeting*, 41–44.

548. Guo, Cheng-ming. 1987. Interactive vocabulary acquisition in XTRA. *IJCAI-87* 2, 715–717.

549. Guy, J.B.M. 1984. An algorithm for identifying cognates between related languages. In *COLING-84*, 448–451.

550. Haas, Andrew. 1987. Parallel parsing for unification grammars. *IJCAI-87* 2, 615–618.

551. Habel, Christopher U., Claus-Rainer Rollinger, Arno Schmidt and Hans-Jochen Schneider. 1980. A logic-oriented approach to automatic text understanding. In *Natural Language Based Computer Systems*, Leonard Bolc, (ed.) Hanser, Munich, 57–117.

552. Habel, Christopher U. 1982. Referential nets with attributes. In *COLING-82*, 101–106.

553. Habel, Christopher U. 1986. Plurals, cardinalities, and structures of determination. In *COLING-86*, 62–64.

554. Haberbeck, Rolf. 1986. A description of the VESPRA speech processing system. In *COLING-86*, 618–620.

555. Haddock, Nicholas J. 1987. Incremental interpretation and combinatory categorial grammar. *IJCAI-87* 2, 661–663.

556. Haduch, Leszek. 1983. L'idée de grammaire avec le contexte naturel. In *ACL Proceedings, First European Conference*, 9–13.

557. Hafner, Carole D. and John D Joyce. 1983.   Using natural language descriptions to improve the usability of databases. In *ACL Proceedings, Conference on Applied Natural Language Processing*, 132–135.

558. Hafner, Carole D. 1984.   Interaction of knowledge sources in a portable natural language interface. In *COLING-84*, 57–60.

559. Hafner, Carole D. 1985.   Semantics of temporal queries and temporal data. In *ACL Proceedings, 23rd Annual Meeting*, 1–8.

560. Hahn, Udo. 1984.   Textual expertise in word experts: an approach to text parsing based on topic/comment monitoring. In *COLING-84*, 402–408.

561. Hahn, Udo and Ulrich Reimer. 1986.   TOPIC essentials. In *COLING-86*, 497–503.

562. Hahn, Udo. 1986.   On lexically distributed text parsing. *ECAI-86* 1, 203–211.

563. Hahn, Walther v., Wolfgang Hoeppner, Anthony Jameson and Wolfgang Wahlster. 1980.   The anatomy of the natural language dialogue system HAM-RPM. In *Natural Language Based Computer Systems*, Leonard Bolc, (ed.) Hanser, Munich, 119–253.

564. Hahn, Walther v. 1986.   Pragmatic considerations in man-machine discourse. In *COLING-86*, 520–526.

565. Hajičová, Eva and Petr Sgall. 1980.   Linguistic Meaning and knowledge representation in automatic understanding of natural language. In *COLING-80*, 67–75.

566. Hajičová, Eva and J Vrbová. 1982.   On the role of the hierarchy of activation in the process of natural language understanding. In *COLING-82*, 107–113.

567. Hajičová, Eva. 1982.   Discussion of Martin Kay's paper. In *Text Processing: Text Analysis and Generation, Text Typology and Attribution*, Sture Allén, (ed.) Almqvist and Wiksell, Stockholm, 359–369.

568. Hajičová, Eva and Petr Sgall. 1983.   Structure of sentence and inferencing in question answering. In *ACL Proceedings, First European Conference*, 21–25.

569. Hajičová, Eva and Petr Sgall. 1984.   From topic and focus of a sentence to linking in a text. In *Computational Models of Natural Language Processing*, Bruno G. Bara and Giovanni Guida, (eds.) North-Holland, Amsterdam, 151–163.

570. Hajičová, Eva and Milena Hnátková. 1984.   Inferencing on linguistically semantic structures. In *COLING-84*, 291–297.

571. Hajičová, Eva and Milena Hnátková. 1984. Linguistically motivated representation of knowledge as a basis for inference procedures. In *Artificial Intelligence and Information-Control Systems of Robots*, Ivan Plander, (ed.) North-Holland, Amsterdam, 167–170.

572. Hajičová, Eva and Petr Sgall. 1985. Towards an automatic identification of topic and focus. In *ACL Proceedings, Second European Conference*, 263–267.

573. Hajičová, Eva and Petr Sgall. 1986. Degrees of understanding. In *COLING-86*, 184–186.

574. Halvorsen, Per-Kristian. 1982. Lexical-functional grammar and order-free semantic composition. In *COLING-82*, 115–120.

575. Halvorsen, Per-Kristian. 1983. Semantics for lexical-functional grammar. *Linguistic Inquiry* 14:4, 567–615.

576. Halvorsen, Per-Kristian. 1986. Natural language understanding and Montague grammar. *Computational Intelligence* 2:1, 54–62.

577. Hamadou, Abelmajid Ben. 1986. A compression technique for Arabic dictionaries: the affix analysis. In *COLING-86*, 286–288.

578. Hanakata, Kenji. 1980. An intelligent digester for interactive text processing. In *COLING-80*, 504–511.

579. Hanakata, Kenji, A. Lesniewski and Shoichi Yokoyama. 1986. Semantic based generation of Japanese German translation system. In *COLING-86*, 560–562.

580. Hankamer, Jorge. 1986. Finite state morphology and left to right phonology. In *Proceedings of the First West Coast Conference on Formal Linguistics*, Mary Dalrymple, Jeffrey Goldberg, Kristin Hanson, Michael Inman, Chris Pinon, and Stephen Wechsler, (ed.) Stanford Linguistics Association, Stanford, 29–34.

581. Harper, Mary P. and Eugene Charniak. 1986. Time and tense in English. In *ACL Proceedings, 24th Annual Meeting*, 3–9.

582. Harris, Larry R. 1980. Prospects for practical natural language systems. In *ACL Proceedings, 18th Annual Meeting*, 129.

583. Harris, Larry R. 1980. ROBOT: a high performance natural language interface for data base query. In *Natural Language Based Computer Systems*, Leonard Bolc, (ed.) Hanser, Munich, 285–318.

584. Harris, Mary Dee. 1985. *Introduction to Natural Language Processing*. Reston Publishing Co., Reston.

585. Harrison, Philip and Michael Maxwell. 1985. Natural language processing at the Boeing company. In *Theoretical Approaches to Natural Language Understanding, a Workshop at Halifax, Nova Scotia*, 131–132.

586. Harrison, Philip and Michael Maxwell. 1986. A new implementation for generalized phrase structure grammar. In *Proceedings of the 6th Canadian Conference on Artificial Intelligence*, 78–83.

587. Hasida, Kôiti. 1986. Conditioned unification for natural language processing. In *COLING-86*, 85–87.

588. Hasida, Kôiti and Syun Isizaki. 1987. Dependency propagation: a unified theory of sentence comprehension and generation. *IJCAI-87* 2, 664–670.

589. Haugeneder, Hans. 1985. An ATN treatment WH-movement. In *ACL Proceedings, Second European Conference*, 41–47.

590. Haugeneder, Hans and Manfred Gehrke. 1986. A user friendly ATN programming environment (APE). In *COLING-86*, 399–401.

591. Hausser, Roland. 1986. *NEWCAT: Parsing Natural Language Using Left-Associative Grammar*. Springer, Berlin.

592. Havens, William S. 1983. Recognition mechanisms for schema-based knowledge representation. *Computers and Mathematics with Applications* 9:1, 185–199.

593. Hayes, Philip J. 1980. Expanding the horizons of natural language interfaces. In *ACL Proceedings, 18th Annual Meeting*, 71–74.

594. Hayes, Philip J. and George V Mouradian. 1980. Flexible parsing. In *ACL Proceedings, 18th Annual Meeting*, 97–103.

595. Hayes, Philip J. 1981. Anaphora for limited domain systems. *IJCAI-81* 1, 416–422.

596. Hayes, Philip J. and Jaime G Carbonell. 1981. Multi-strategy construction-specific parsing for flexible data base query and update. *IJCAI-81* 1, 432–439.

597. Hayes, Philip J. 1981. A construction-specific approach to focused interaction in flexible parsing. In *ACL Proceedings, 19th Annual Meeting*, 149–152.

598. Hayes, Philip J. and George V Mouradian. 1981. Flexible parsing. *American Journal of Computational Linguistics* 7:4, 232–242.

599. Hayes, Philip J. and Jaime G Carbonell. 1983. Natural language tutorial. In *IJCAI-83, Tutorial on Artificial Intelligence*, 1–39.

600. Hayes, Philip J. and Jaime G Carbonell. 1983. A framework for processing corrections in task-oriented dialogues. In *IJCAI-83*, 668–670.

601. Hayes, Philip J. 1984. Entity-oriented parsing. In *COLING-84*, 212–217.

602. Hayes, Philip J., Peggy M. Anderson and Scott Safier. 1985. Semantic caseframe parsing and syntactic generality. In *ACL Proceedings, 23rd Annual Meeting*, 153–160.

603. Hayes, Philip J., Alexander G. Hauptmann, Jaime G. Carbonell and Masaru Tomita. 1986. Parsing spoken language: a semantic caseframe approach. In *COLING-86*, 587-592.

604. Hays, David G. 1982. 2002: another score. In *ACL Proceedings, 20th Annual Meeting*, 95-96.

605. Heidorn, George E. 1982. Experience with an easily computed metric for ranking alternative parses. In *ACL Proceedings, 20th Annual Meeting*, 82-84.

606. Hein, A.S. 1982. An experimental parser. In *COLING-82*, 121-126.

607. Helbig, Hermann. 1984. Natural language access to the data base of the AIDOS/VS information retrieval system. In *Artificial Intelligence and Information-Control Systems of Robots*, Ivan Plander, (ed.) North-Holland, Amsterdam, 171-174.

608. Hellwig, Peter. 1980. PLAIN - a program system for dependency analysis and for simulating natural language inference. In *Representation and Processing of Natural Language*, Leonard Bolc, (ed.) Hanser, Munich, 271-376.

609. Hellwig, Peter. 1986. Dependency unification grammar. In *COLING-86*, 195-198.

610. Hendrix, Gary G. 1986 (1978). Semantic aspects of translation. In *Readings in Natural Language Processing*, Barbara J. Grosz, Karen Sparck-Jones and Bonnie Lynn Webber, (eds.) Morgan Kaufmann, Los Altos, 267-283.

611. Hendrix, Gary G., Earl Sacerdoti, D. Sagalowicz and Jonathan Slocum. 1986 (1978). Developing a natural language interface to complex data. In *Readings in Natural Language Processing*, Barbara J. Grosz, Karen Sparck-Jones and Bonnie Lynn Webber, (eds.) Morgan Kaufmann, Los Altos, 563-584.

612. Hendrix, Gary G. 1980. Future Prospects for computational linguistics. In *ACL Proceedings, 18th Annual Meeting*, 131-135.

613. Hendrix, Gary G. and William H Lewis. 1981. Transportable natural-language interfaces to databases. In *ACL Proceedings, 19th Annual Meeting*, 159-165.

614. Hendrix, Gary G. 1982. Natural language interface. *American Journal of Computational Linguistics* 8:2, 56-61.

615. Hendrix, Gary G. 1986. Q & A: already a success ?. In *COLING-86*, 164-166.

616. Hendrix, Gary G. 1986. Bringing natural language processing to the micro-computer market: the story of Q & A. In *ACL Proceedings, 24th Annual Meeting*, 2.

617. Herskovits, Annette. 1980. On the spatial use of prepositions. In *ACL Proceedings, 18th Annual Meeting*, 1–5.

618. Herskovits, Annette. 1986. *Language and Spatial Cognition: An Interdisciplinary Study of the Prepositions in English*. Cambridge University Press, Cambridge.

619. Hess, Michael. 1985. How does natural language quantify?. In *ACL Proceedings, Second European Conference*, 8–15.

620. Hess, Michael. 1985. About the role of control information in natural language question answering systems. In *Natural Language Understanding and Logic Programming*, Veronica Dahl and Patrick Saint-Dizier, (eds.) North-Holland, Amsterdam, 165–180.

621. Hiltz, Starr R., Kenneth Johnson and Ann Marie Rabke. 1980. The process of communication in face to face vs. computational conferences. In *ACL Proceedings, 18th Annual Meeting*, 75–79.

622. Hindle, Donald. 1983. Deterministic parsing of syntactic non-fluencies. In *ACL Proceedings, 21st Annual Meeting*, 123–128.

623. Hinrichs, Erhard W. 1986. A compositional semantics for directional modifiers - locative case reopened. In *COLING-86*, 347–349.

624. Hinrichs, Erhard W. 1987. A compositional semantics of temporal expressions in English. In *ACL Proceedings, 25th Annual Meeting*, 8–15.

625. Hiraga, Yuzuru, Yoshihiko Ono and Yamada Hisao. 1980. An analysis of the standard English keyboard. In *COLING-80*, 242–248.

626. Hiraga, Yuzuru, Yoshihiko Ono and Yamada Hisao. 1980. An assignment of key-codes for a Japanese character keyboard. In *COLING-80*, 249–256.

627. Hirschberg, Julia. 1984. Toward a redefinition of yes/no questions. In *COLING-84*, 48–51.

628. Hirschberg, Julia and Janet B Pierrehumbert. 1986. The intonational structuring of discourse. In *ACL Proceedings, 24th Annual Meeting*, 136–144.

629. Hirschberg, Julia, Diane J. Litman, Janet B. Pierrehumbert and G Ward. 1987. Intonation and the structure of discourse. *IJCAI-87* 2, 636–639.

630. Hirschberg, Julia. 1987. Untitled. In *TINLAP-3*, 86–92.

631. Hirschberg, Julia and Diane J Litman. 1987. Now let's talk about now: identifying cue phrases intonationally. In *ACL Proceedings, 25th Annual Meeting*, 163–171.

632. Hirschman, Lynette and Guy Story. 1981. Representing implicit and explicit time relations in narrative. *IJCAI-81* 1, 289–295.

633. Hirschman, Lynette and Karl Puder. 1982. Restriction grammar in PROLOG. In *Proceedings of the First International Conference on Logic Programming*, Michel Van Caneghem, (ed.) Assocation pour la diffusion et le développement de PROLOG, Marseille, 85–90.

634. Hirschman, Lynette and Karl Puder. 1986. Restriction grammar: A PROLOG implementation. In *Logic Programming and its Applications (Volume 2)*, Michel van Canegham and David H.D. Warren, (eds.) Ablex, Norwood, New Jersey, 00–00.

635. Hirst, Graeme. 1981. Discourse-oriented anaphora resolution: a review. *American Journal of Computational Linguistics* 7:2, 85–98.

636. Hirst, Graeme. 1981. *Anaphora in Natural Language Understanding: A Survey*. Springer, Berlin.

637. Hirst, Graeme and Eugene Charniak. 1982. Word sense and case slot disambiguation. In *AAAI-82*, 95–98.

638. Hirst, Graeme. 1983. A foundation for semantic interpretation. In *ACL Proceedings, 21st Annual Meeting*, 64–73.

639. Hirst, Graeme. 1984. A semantic process for syntactic disambiguation. In *AAAI-84*, 148–152.

640. Hirst, Graeme. 1986. *Semantic Interpretation and the Resolution of Ambiguity*. Cambridge University Press, Cambridge.

641. Hitaka, Toru and Sho Yoshida. 1980. A syntax parser based on the case dependency grammar and its efficiency. In *COLING-80*, 15–20.

642. Hobbs, Jerry R. 1986 (1978). Resolving pronoun references. In *Readings in Natural Language Processing*, Barbara J. Grosz, Karen Sparck-Jones and Bonnie Lynn Webber, (eds.) Morgan Kaufmann, Los Altos, 339–352.

643. Hobbs, Jerry R. 1980. Interactive discourse: influences of the social context. In *ACL Proceedings, 18th Annual Meeting*, 65–66.

644. Hobbs, Jerry R. 1980. Selective inference. In *Proceedings of the Third Biennial Conference of the Canadian Society for Computational Studies of Intelligence (3rd Canadian Conference on AI)*, 101–114.

645. Hobbs, Jerry R. and Michael Agar. 1981. Text plans and world plans in natural discourse. *IJCAI-81* 1, 190–196.

646. Hobbs, Jerry R. 1981. Metaphor interpretation as selective inferencing. *IJCAI-81* 1, 85–91.

647. Hobbs, Jerry R., Donald E. Walker and Robert A Amsler. 1982. Natural language access to structured text. In *COLING-82*, 127–132.

648. Hobbs, Jerry R. 1982. Towards an understanding of coherence in discourse. In *Strategies for Natural Language Processing*, Wendy G. Lehnert and Martin H. Ringle, (eds.) Erlbaum, Hillsdale, 223–243.

649. Hobbs, Jerry R. 1983. An improper treatment of quantification in ordinary English. In *ACL Proceedings, 21st Annual Meeting*, 57–63.

650. Hobbs, Jerry R. 1984. Building a large knowledge base for a natural language system. In *COLING-84*, 283–286.

651. Hobbs, Jerry R. 1985. Ontological promiscuity. In *ACL Proceedings, 23rd Annual Meeting*, 61–69.

652. Hobbs, Jerry R., William Croft, Todd Davies, Douglas Edwards and Kenneth Laws. 1986. Commonsense metaphysics and lexical semantics. In *ACL Proceedings, 24th Annual Meeting*, 231–240.

653. Hobbs, Jerry R. 1987. World knowledge and world meaning. In *TINLAP-3*, 20–25.

654. Hobbs, Jerry R. and Stuart M Shieber. 1987. An algorithm for generating quantifier scopings. *Computational Linguistics* 13:1–2, 47–63.

655. Hoch, Dietrich and Winfried Heicking. 1980. Syntactic-semantic analysis of German sentences. In *Representation and Processing of Natural Language*, Leonard Bolc, (ed.) Hanser, Munich, 207–270.

656. Hoenkamp, Edward. 1980. Spontaneous speech as a feedback process. In *AISB-80*, 142–146.

657. Hoeppner, Wolfgang. 1982. A multilayered approach to the handling of word formation. In *COLING-82*, 133–138.

658. Hoeppner, Wolfgang, Thomas Christaller, Heinz Marburger, Katharina Morik, Bernhard Nebel, Mike O'Leary and Wolfgang Wahlster. 1983. Beyond domain-independence: experience with the development of a German language access system to highly diverse background systems. In *IJCAI-83*, 588–594.

659. Hofman, Th.R. 1980. On the derivation of a conversational maxim. In *COLING-80*, 236–239.

660. Hogan, Douglas L. 1983. Speech interfaces. In *ACL Proceedings, Conference on Applied Natural Language Processing*, 178–179.

661. Hollander, Clifford R. 1980. Use of an attribute grammar in network-based representation schemes. In *Proceedings of the Third Biennial Conference of the Canadian Society for Computational Studies of Intelligence (3rd Canadian Conference on AI)*, 95–100.

662. Hori, Koichi, Seinosuke Toda and Hisashi Yasunaga. 1986. Learning the space of word meanings for information retrieval systems. In *COLING-86*, 374–379.

663. Hovy, Eduard H. and Roger C Schank. 1984. Language generation by computer. In *Computational Models of Natural Language Processing*, Bruno G. Bara and Giovanni Guida, (eds.) North-Holland, Amsterdam, 165–195.

664. Hovy, Eduard H. 1985. Integrating text planning and production in generation. *IJCAI-85* 2, 848–851.

665. Hovy, Eduard H. 1987. Interpretation in generation. In *AAAI-87*, 545–549.

666. Huang, Xiuming. 1983. Dealing with conjunctions in a machine translation environment. In *ACL Proceedings, First European Conference*, 81–85.

667. Huang, Xiuming. 1984. Dealing with conjunction in a machine translation environment. In *COLING-84*, 243–246.

668. Huang, Xiuming and Louise Guthrie. 1986. Parsing in parallel. In *COLING-86*, 140–145.

669. Huettner, Alison K., Marie M. Vaughan and David D McDonald. 1987. Constraints on the generation of adjunct clauses. In *ACL Proceedings, 25th Annual Meeting*, 207–214.

670. Hull, Jonathan J. 1986. Inter-world constraints in visual word recognition. In *Proceedings of the 6th Canadian Conference on Artificial Intelligence*, 134–138.

671. Hurum, Sven O. and Lenhart K Schubert. 1986. Two types of quantifier scoping. In *Proceedings of the 6th Canadian Conference on Artificial Intelligence*, 39–43.

672. Hussman, Michael, Martin Bode, Michael Borowiak, Peter Schefe and Bernd Wronn. 1984. Extending the natural language system SWYSS by a functional database. In *ECAI-84*, 217–220.

673. Hutchins, W. John. 1986. *Machine Translation: Past, Present, Future*. Ellis Horwood/Wiley, Chichester/New York.

674. Huttenlocher, Daniel P. and Victor W Zue. 1983. Phonotactic and lexical constraints in speech recognition. In *AAAI-83*, 172–176.

675. Hyvönen, Eero. 1983. Graph grammar approach to natural language parsing and understanding. In *IJCAI-83*, 671–674.

676. Hyvönen, Eero. 1984. Semantic parsing as graph language transformation: a multidimensional approach to parsing highly inflectional languages. In *COLING-84*, 517–520.

677. Iida, Hitoshi, Kentaro Ogura and Hirosato Nomura. 1984. A case analysis method cooperation with ATNG and its application to machine translation. In *COLING-84*, 154–158.

678. Isabelle, Pierre. 1984. Another look at nominal compounds. In *COLING-84*, 509–516.

679. Isabelle, Pierre and Laurent Bourbeau. 1985. TAUM-AVIATION: its technical features and some experimental results.. *Computational Linguistics* 11:1, 18–27.

680. Isabelle, Pierre and Elliott Macklovitch. 1986. Transfer and MT modularity. In *COLING-86*, 115–117.

681. Isahara, Hitoshi and Shun Ishizaki. 1986. Context analysis system for Japanese text. In *COLING-86*, 244–246.

682. Isard, Stephen. 1986. Speech synthesis and recognition. In *Artificial Intelligence: Principles and Applications*, Masoud Yazdani, (ed.) Chapman and Hall, London, 111–121.

683. Ishimoto, A. 1982. A Lesniewskian version of Montague grammar. In *COLING-82*, 139–144.

684. Ishizaki, Shun. 1983. Generation of Japanese sentences from conceptual representation. In *IJCAI-83*, 613–615.

685. Isoda, Michio, Hideo Aiso, Noriyuki Kamibayashi and Yoshifumi Matsunaga. 1986. Model for lexical knowledge base. In *COLING-86*, 451–453.

686. Israel, David J. 1983. A prolegomenon to situation semantics. In *ACL Proceedings, 21st Annual Meeting*, 28–37.

687. Israel, David J. 1983. Interpreting network formalisms. *Computers and Mathematics with Applications* 9:1, 1–13.

688. Israel, David J. 1987. On formal versus commonsense semantics. In *TINLAP-3*, 115–118.

689. Izumida, Yoshio, Hiroshi Ishikawa, Toshiaki Yoshino, Tadashi Hoshiai and Akifumi Makinouch. 1985. A natural language interface using a world model. In *ACL Proceedings, Second European Conference*, 205–212.

690. Jacobs, Paul S. 1983. Generation in a natural language interface. In *IJCAI-83*, 610–612.

691. Jacobs, Paul S. and Lisa F Rau. 1984. Ace: associating language with meaning. In *ECAI-84*, 137–146.

692. Jacobs, Paul S. and Lisa F Rau. 1985. Ace: associating language with meaning. In *Advances in Artificial Intelligence*, Tim O'Shea, (ed.) North-Holland, Amsterdam, 295–304.

693. Jacobs, Paul S. 1985. PHRED: a generator for natural language interfaces. *Computational Linguistics* 11:4, 219–242.

694. Jacobs, Paul S. 1986. Knowledge structures for natural language generation. In *COLING-86*, 554–559.

695. Jacobs, Paul S. 1986. The KING natural language generator. *ECAI-86* 1, 193–202.

696. Jacobs, Paul S. 1987. A knowledge framework for natural language analysis. *IJCAI-87* 2, 675–678.

697. Jameson, Anthony and Wolfgang Wahlster. 1982. User modelling in anaphora generation: ellipsis and definite description. In *ECAI-82*, 222–227.

698. Jameson, Anthony. 1983. Impression monitoring in evaluation-oriented dialog - the role of the listener's assumed expectations and the values in the generation of informative statements. In *IJCAI-83*, 616–620.

699. Jansen-Winkeln, Roman M. 1987. LEGAS: inductive learning of grammatical structures. In *Advances in Artificial Intelligence (Proceedings of AISB-87)*, Christopher S. Mellish and John Hallam, (eds.) Wiley, Chichester, 169–181.

700. Jaspaert, Lieven. 1986. Linguistic developments in EUROTRA since 1983. In *COLING-86*, 294–296.

701. Jäppinen, Harri, Aarno Lehtola, Esa Nelimarkka and Matti Ylilammi. 1983. Knowledge engineering approach to morphological analysis. In *ACL Proceedings, First European Conference*, 49–51.

702. Jäppinen, Harri, Aarno Lehtola and K. Valkonen. 1986. Functional structures for parsing dependency constraints. In *COLING-86*, 461–463.

703. Jäppinen, Harri and Matti Ylilammi. 1986. Associative model of morphological analysis: an empirical enquiry. *Computational Linguistics* 12:4, 257–272.

704. Jean-Claude, Bassano. 1986. DIALECT: an expert assistant for information retrieval. In *Proceedings of the 6th Canadian Conference on Artificial Intelligence*, 199–203.

705. Jensen, Karen, George E. Heidorn, Lance A. Miller and Yael Ravin. 1983. Parse fitting and prose fixing: getting a hold on ill-formedness. *American Journal of Computational Linguistics* 9:3–4, 147–160.

706. Jensen, Karen and George E Heidorn. 1983. The 'fitted' parse: 100% parsing capability in a syntactic grammar of English. In *ACL Proceedings, Conference on Applied Natural Language Processing*, 93–98.

707. Jin, Wanying. 1986. Machine translation between Chinese and English. In *Proceedings of the 6th Canadian Conference on Artificial Intelligence*, 129–133.

708. Johnson, Caroll and Joan Bachenko. 1982. Applied computational linguistics in perspective. *American Journal of Computational Linguistics* 8:2, 55, 83–84.

709. Johnson, Mark. 1984. A discovery algorithm for certain phonological rules. In *COLING-84*, 344–347.

710. Johnson, Mark. 1985. Computer aids for comparative dictionaries. *Linguistics* 23:2, 285–302.

711. Johnson, Mark. 1985. Parsing with discontinuous constituents. In *ACL Proceedings, 23rd Annual Meeting*, 127–132.

712. Johnson, Mark and Ewan Klein. 1986. Discourse, anaphora and parsing. In *COLING-86*, 669–675.

713. Johnson, Philip N. and Wendy G Lehnert. 1986. Beyond exploratory programming: a methodology and environment for conceptual natural language processing. *AAAI-86* 1, 594–600.

714. Johnson, Rod L. 1983. Parsing with transition networks. In *Parsing Natural Language*, Margaret King, (ed.) Academic Press, London, 59–72.

715. Johnson, Rod L. 1983. Parsing - an MT perspective. In *Automatic Natural Language Parsing*, Karen Sparck-Jones and Yorick A. Wilks, (eds.) Ellis Horwood/Wiley, Chichester/New York, 32–38.

716. Johnson, Rod L., Steven Krauwer, Michael A. Rosner and G.B Varile. 1984. The design of the kernel architecture of the EUROTRA system. In *COLING-84*, 226–235.

717. Johnson, Rod L. 1985. Machine translation. In *Proceedings of the Alvey/ICL Workshop on Linguistic Theory and Computer Applications*, Peter Whitelock, Harold Somers, Paul Bennett, Rod L. Johnson and Mary McGee Wood, (eds.) CCL/UMIST, Manchester, 169–189.

718. Johnson, Rod L. and Peter Whitelock. 1987. Machine translation as an expert task. In *Machine Translation: Theoretical and Methodological Issues*, Sergei Nirenberg, (ed.) Cambridge University Press, Cambridge, 136–144.

719. Johnson, Tim. 1985. *Natural Language Computing: the Commercial Implications*. Ovum, London.

720. Johnson-Laird, Philip N. 1981. Cognition, computers and mental models. *Cognition* 10, 139–144.

721. Johnson-Laird, Philip N. 1981. Mental models of meaning. In *Elements of Discourse Understanding*, Aravind K. Joshi, Bonnie Lynn Webber and Ivan Sag, (eds.) Cambridge University Press, Cambridge, 106–126.

722. Johnson-Laird, Philip N. 1983. *Mental Models*. Cambridge University Press, Cambridge.

723. Johnson-Laird, Philip N. 1984. Semantic primitives or meaning postulates: mental models of propositional representations. In *Computational Models of Natural Language Processing*, Bruno G. Bara and Giovanni Guida, (eds.) North-Holland, Amsterdam, 227–246.

724. Johnstone, Anne and Gerry Altmann. 1985. Automated speech recognition: a framework for research. In *ACL Proceedings, Second European Conference*, 239–243.

725. Jones, Mark A. and David S Warren. 1982. Conceptual dependency and Montague grammar: a step toward conciliation. In *AAAI-82*, 79–83.

726. Jones, Mark A. 1983. Activation-based parsing. In *IJCAI-83*, 678–682.

727. Jones, Mark A. and Alan S Driscoll. 1985. Movement in active production networks. In *ACL Proceedings, 23rd Annual Meeting*, 161–166.

728. Jones, Mark A. 1987. Feedback as a coindexing mechanism in connectionist architectures. *IJCAI-87* 2, 602–610.

729. Joshi, Aravind K. 1980. Influence of the problem context. In *ACL Proceedings, 18th Annual Meeting*, 31–33.

730. Joshi, Aravind K. and Leon S Levy. 1980. Phrase structure trees bear more fruit than you would have thought. In *ACL Proceedings, 18th Annual Meeting*, 41–42.

731. Joshi, Aravind K., Bonnie Lynn Webber and Ivan A. Sag, (eds.) 1981. *Elements of Discourse Understanding*. Cambridge University Press, Cambridge.

732. Joshi, Aravind K. 1982. Processing of sentences with intrasentential code-switching. In *COLING-82*, 145–150.

733. Joshi, Aravind K. 1982. Twenty years of reflections. In *ACL Proceedings, 20th Annual Meeting*, 102.

734. Joshi, Aravind K. and Leon S Levy. 1982. Phrase structure trees bear more fruit than you would have thought. *American Journal of Computational Linguistics* 8:1, 1–11.

735. Joshi, Aravind K. 1983. Factoring recursion and dependencies.. In *ACL Proceedings, 21st Annual Meeting*, 7–15.

736. Joshi, Aravind K. 1983. Domain-independent natural language interfaces. In *ACL Proceedings, Conference on Applied Natural Language Processing*, 1–2.

737. Joshi, Aravind K., Bonnie Lynn Webber and Ralph M Weischedel. 1984. Preventing false inferences. In *COLING-84*, 134–138.

738. Joshi, Aravind K., Bonnie Lynn Webber and Ralph M Weischedel. 1984. Living up to expectations: computing expert responses. In *AAAI-84*, 169–175.

739. Joshi, Aravind K. 1985. Processing of sentences with intrasentential code switching. In *Natural Language Parsing*, David R. Dowty, Lauri Karttunen and Arnold M. Zwicky, (eds.) Cambridge University Press, Cambridge, 190–205.

740. Joshi, Aravind K. 1985. Tree adjoining grammars: how much context-sensitivity is required to provide reasonable structural descriptions?. In *Natural Language Parsing*, David R. Dowty, Lauri Karttunen and Arnold M. Zwicky, (eds.) Cambridge University Press, Cambridge, 206–250.

741. Joshi, Aravind K. and K Vijay-Shanker. 1985. Some computational properties of tree adjoining grammars. In *ACL Proceedings, 23rd Annual Meeting*, 82–93.

742. Joshi, Aravind K. 1987. Word-order variation in natural language generation. In *AAAI-87*, 550–555.

743. Joshi, Aravind K. 1987. Unification and some new grammatical formalism. In *TINLAP-3*, 43–48.

744. Joshi, Aravind K. 1987. Generation - a new frontier of natural language processing?. In *TINLAP-3*, 181–184.

745. Kac, Michael B. and Alexis Manaster-Ramer. 1986. Parsing without (much) phrase structure. In *COLING-86*, 156–158.

746. Kac, Michael B., Tom Rindflesch and Karen L Ryan. 1986. Reconnaissance-attack parsing. In *COLING-86*, 159–160.

747. Kac, Michael B., Alexis Manaster-Ramer and William C Rounds. 1987. Simultaneous-distributive coordination and context-freeness. *Computational Linguistics* 13:1–2, 25–30.

748. Kahn, Kenneth M. 1984. A grammar kit in PROLOG. In *New Horizons in Educational Computing*, Masoud Yazdani, (ed.) Ellis Horwood/Wiley, Chichester/New York, 178–189.

749. Kakizaki, Takahiro. 1986. Research and development of electronic dictionary for natural language processing. *ICOT Journal* 14, 9–16.

750. Kalish, Candace and Matthew Cox. 1987. Porting an extensible natural language interface: a case history. In *AAAI-87*, 556–560.

751. Kalita, Jugal K., M.J. Colbourn and Gordon I McCalla. 1984. A response to the need for summary responses. In *COLING-84*, 432–436.

752. Kalita, Jugal K., Marlene L. Jones and Gordon I McCalla. 1986. Summarizing natural language database responses. *Computational Linguistics* 12:2, 107–124.

753. Kameyama, Megumi. 1986. A property-sharing constraint in centering. In *ACL Proceedings, 24th Annual Meeting*, 200–206.

754. Kaplan, Ronald M. 1981. A view of parsing. In *ACL Proceedings, 19th Annual Meeting*, 103–104.

755. Kaplan, Ronald M. 1985. Three seductions of computational psycholinguistics. In *Proceedings of the Alvey/ICL Workshop on Linguistic Theory and Computer Applications*, Peter Whitelock, Harold Somers, Paul Bennett, Rod L. Johnson and Mary McGee Wood, (eds.) CCL/UMIST, Manchester, 95–119.

756. Kaplan, Ronald M. 1985. Lexical-functional grammar vs. logic grammar. In *Theoretical Approaches to Natural Language Understanding, a Workshop at Halifax, Nova Scotia*, 13.

757. Kaplan, S. Jerrold. 1981. Appropriate responses to inappropriate questions. In *Elements of Discourse Understanding*, Aravind K. Joshi, Bonnie Lynn Webber and Ivan Sag, (eds.) Cambridge University Press, Cambridge, 127–144.

758. Kaplan, S. Jerrold and James Davidson. 1981. Interpreting natural language database updates. In *ACL Proceedings, 19th Annual Meeting*, 139–141.

759. Kaplan, S. Jerrold. 1982. Cooperative responses from a portable natural language query system. *Artificial Intelligence* 19:2, 165–187.

760. Kaplan, S. Jerrold. 1983. The impact of natural language access on database design and implementation. In *ACL Proceedings, Conference on Applied Natural Language Processing*, 198.

761. Kaplan, S. Jerrold. 1983. Cooperative responses from a portable natural language database query system. In *Computational Models of Discourse*, Michael Brady and Robert C. Berwick, (eds.) MIT Press, Cambridge, Ma., 167–208.

762. Karlsson, Fred. 1985. Automatic hyphenation of Finnish. In *Computational Morphosyntax: Report on Research 1981-1984*, Fred Karlsson, (ed.) University of Helsinki, Helsinki, 93–114.

763. Karlsson, Fred. 1985. Morphological tagging of Finnish. In *Computational Morphosyntax: Report on Research 1981-1984*, Fred Karlsson, (ed.) University of Helsinki, Helsinki, 115–136.

764. Karlsson, Fred. 1985. Parsing Finnish in terms of process grammar. In *Computational Morphosyntax: Report on Research 1981-1984*, Fred Karlsson, (ed.) University of Helsinki, Helsinki, 137–173.

765. Karlsson, Fred. 1986. A paradigm-based morphological analyzer. In *Papers from the Fifth Scandinavian Conference of Computational Linguistics*, Fred Karlsson, (ed.) University of Helsinki, Helsinki, 95–112.

766. Karttunen, Lauri. 1983. KIMMO: a general morphological processor. *Texas Linguistic Forum* 22, 165–186.

767. Karttunen, Lauri and Kent Wittenburg. 1983. A two-level morphological analysis of English. *Texas Linguistic Forum* 22, 217–228.

768. Karttunen, Lauri. 1984. Features and values. In *COLING-84*, 28–33.

769. Karttunen, Lauri and Arnold M Zwicky. 1985. Natural language parsing: introduction. In *Natural Language Parsing*, David R. Dowty, Lauri Karttunen and Arnold M. Zwicky, (eds.) Cambridge University Press, Cambridge, 1–25.

770. Karttunen, Lauri and Martin Kay. 1985. Parsing in a free word order language. In *Natural Language Parsing*, David R. Dowty, Lauri Karttunen and Arnold M. Zwicky, (eds.) Cambridge University Press, Cambridge, 279–306.

771. Karttunen, Lauri and Martin Kay. 1985. Structure sharing with binary trees. In *ACL Proceedings, 23rd Annual Meeting*, 133–136.

772. Karttunen, Lauri. 1986. D-PATR: a development environment for unification-based grammars. In *COLING-86*, 74–80.

773. Kashket, Michael B. 1986. Parsing a free-word order language: Warlpiri. In *ACL Proceedings, 24th Annual Meeting*, 60–66.

774. Kasper, Robert and William Rounds. 1986. A logical semantics for feature structures. In *ACL Proceedings, 24th Annual Meeting*, 257–266.

775. Kasper, Robert. 1987. A unification method for disjunctive feature descritpions. In *ACL Proceedings, 25th Annual Meeting*, 235–242.

776. Kawada, Tsutomu, Shin-ya Amano and Kunio Sakai. 1980. Linguistic error correction of Japanese sentences. In *COLING-80*, 257–261.

777. Kawaguchi, Atsuo, Naoki Taoka, Riichiro Mizoguchi, Takahira Yamaguchi and Osamu Kakusho. 1986. An intelligent interview system for conceptual schema design of relational database. *ECAI-86* 2, 39–45.

778. Kay, Martin. 1986 (1980). Algorithm schemata and data structures in syntactic processing. In *Readings in Natural Language Processing*, Barbara J. Grosz, Karen Sparck-Jones and Bonnie Lynn Webber, (eds.) Morgan Kaufmann, Los Altos, 35–70.

779. Kay, Martin. 1986 (1982). Parsing in functional unification grammar. In *Readings in Natural Language Processing*, Barbara J. Grosz, Karen Sparck-Jones and Bonnie Lynn Webber, (eds.) Morgan Kaufmann, Los Altos, 125–138.

780. Kay, Martin. 1982. Algorithm schemata and data structures in syntactic processing. In *Text Processing: Text Analysis and Generation, Text Typology and Attribution*, Sture Allén, (ed.) Almqvist and Wiksell, Stockholm, 327–358.

781. Kay, Martin. 1982. Machine translation. *American Journal of Computational Linguistics* 8:2, 74–78.

782. Kay, Martin. 1983. When meta-rules are not meta-rules. In *Automatic Natural Language Parsing*, Karen Sparck-Jones and Yorick A. Wilks, (eds.) Ellis Horwood/Wiley, Chichester/New York, 94–116.

783. Kay, Martin. 1984. Functional unification grammar: a formalism for machine translation. In *COLING-84*, 75–78.

784. Kay, Martin. 1984. The dictionary server. In *COLING-84*, 461.

785. Kay, Martin. 1985. Parsing in functional unification grammar. In *Natural Language Parsing*, David R. Dowty, Lauri Karttunen and Arnold M. Zwicky, (eds.) Cambridge University Press, Cambridge, 251–278.

786. Kay, Martin. 1985. Unification in grammar. In *Natural Language Understanding and Logic Programming*, Veronica Dahl and Patrick Saint-Dizier, (eds.) North-Holland, Amsterdam, 233–240.

787. Kay, Martin. 1986. Machine translation will not work. In *ACL Proceedings, 24th Annual Meeting*, 268.

788. Kay, Martin. 1987. The linguistic connection. In *TINLAP-3*, 49–55.

789. Kayser, Daniel and Daniel Coulon. 1981. Variable-depth natural language understanding. *IJCAI-81* 1, 64–66.

790. Kegl, Judy. 1987. The boundary between word knowledge and world knowledge. In *TINLAP-3*, 26–31.

791. Kehler, T.P. and R.C Woods. 1980. ATN grammar modeling in applied linguistics. In *ACL Proceedings, 18th Annual Meeting*, 123–126.

792. Keirsey, David M. 1982. Word learning with hierarchy-guided inference. In *AAAI-82*, 99–102.

793. Kempen, Gerard and Edward Hoenkamp. 1982. Incremental sentence generation: implications for the structure of a syntactic processor. In *COLING-82*, 151–156.

794. Kempen, Gerard and Pieter Huijbers. 1983. The lexicalisation process in sentence, production and naming: indirect election of words. *Cognition* 14, 185–210.

795. Kempen, Gerard. 1987. A framework for incremental syntactic tree formation. *IJCAI-87* 2, 655–660.

796. Kettunen, Kimmo. 1986. On modelling dependency-oriented parsing. In *Papers from the Fifth Scandinavian Conference of Computational Linguistics*, Fred Karlsson, (ed.) University of Helsinki, Helsinki, 113–120.

797. Khan, Robert, Jocelyn S. Liu, Tatsuo Ito and Kelly Shuldberg. 1983. KIMMO user's manual. *Texas Linguistic Forum* 22, 203–215.

798. Khan, Robert. 1983. A two-level morphological analysis of Rumanian. *Texas Linguistic Forum* 22, 253–270.

799. Kiefer, Ference. 1980. Topic-comment structure of texts (and its contribution to the automatic processing of texts). In *COLING-80*, 240–241.

800. Kilbury, James. 1984. GPSG-based parsing and generation. In *Probleme des (Text-) Verstehens - Ansätze der Künstlichen Intelligenz*, Claus-Rainer Rollinger, (ed.) Max Niemeyer, Tübingen, 67–76.

801. Kilbury, James. 1985. A modification of the Earley-Shieber algorithm for direct parsing of ID/LP grammars. In *GWAI-84: 8th German Workshop on Artificial Intelligence*, Joachim Laubsch, (ed.) Springer, Heidelberg, 39–48.

802. Kilbury, James. 1985. Chart parsing and the Earley algorithm. In *Kontextfreie Syntaxen und verwandte Systeme*, Ursula Klenk, (ed.) Max Niemeyer, Tübingen.

803. Kilbury, James. 1986. Category cooccurrence restriction and the elimination of metarules. In *COLING-86*, 50–55.

804. Kilbury, James. 1986. Language variation, parsing, and the modelling of users' language varieties. *ECAI-86* 2, 29–32.

805. King, Margaret. 1981. Design characteristics of a machine translation system. *IJCAI-81* 1, 43–46.

806. King, Margaret. 1983. Transformational parsing. In *Parsing Natural Language*, Margaret King, (ed.) Academic Press, London, 19–34.

807. King, Margaret, (ed.) 1983. *Parsing Natural Language*. Academic Press, London.

808. King, Margaret. 1984. When is the next ALPAC report due?. In *COLING-84*, 352–353.

809. King, Margaret. 1986. The prospects of machine translation. *ECAI-86* 1, 181–192.

810. King, Margaret. 1986. Machine translation already does work. In *ACL Proceedings, 24th Annual Meeting*, 269–270.

811. King, Paul L. 1980. Human factors and linguistic considerations: keys to high-speed Chinese character input. In *COLING-80*, 279–282.

812. Kinukawa, Hiroshi, Hiroshi Matsuoka and Mutsuko Kimura. 1980. Japanese sentence analysis for automatic indexing. In *COLING-80*, 514–519.

813. Kirschner, Z. 1982. On a device in dictionary operations in machine translation. In *COLING-82*, 157–160.

814. Kitagawa, Toshio. 1981. Extensionality and intensionality in the processing system of intelligent information. In *Formal Approaches to Natural Language*, Shogo Iguchi, (ed.) Kyoto Working Group of Montague Grammar, Kyoto, 159–168.

815. Kitazawa, Shigeyoshi, Masa-aki Ishikawa and Shuji Doshita. 1985. DP-matching: with or without phonemes?. *IJCAI-85* 2, 883–885.

816. Kittredge, Richard. 1980. Embedded sublanguages and natural language processing. In *COLING-80*, 209–210.

817. Kittredge, Richard. 1980. Natural language queries for a linguistic data base using PROLOG. In *Proceedings of the Third Biennial Conference of the Canadian Society for Computational Studies of Intelligence (3rd Canadian Conference on AI)*, 151–157.

818. Kittredge, Richard I. 1982. Sublanguages. *American Journal of Computational Linguistics* 8:2, 79–82.

819. Kittredge, Richard I. and Igor Mel'čuk. 1983. Towards a computable model of meaning-text relations within a natural sublanguage. In *IJCAI-83*, 657–659.

820. Kittredge, Richard I. 1983. Semantic processing of texts in restricted sublanguages. *Computers and Mathematics with Applications* 9:1, 45–58.

821. Kittredge, Richard I., A. Polguère and E Goldberg. 1986. Synthesizing weather forecasts from formatted data. In *COLING-86*, 563–565.

822. Kittredge, Richard I., A. Polguère and E Goldberg. 1986. Natural language report synthesis: an application to marine weather forecasts. In *Proceedings of the 6th Canadian Conference on Artificial Intelligence*, 67–70.

823. Kittredge, Richard I. 1987. The significance of sublanguage for automatic translation. In *Machine Translation: Theoretical and Methodological Issues*, Sergei Nirenberg, (ed.) Cambridge University Press, Cambridge, 59–67.

824. Klahr, Philip, Larry Travis and Charles Kellogg. 1980. A deductive system for natural language question answering. In *Natural Language Question Answering Systems*, Leonard Bolc, (ed.) Hanser, Munich, 73–136.

825. Klein, Ewan H. 1987. DRT in unification categorial grammar. In *Proceedings of the Alvey Sponsored Workshop on Formal Semantics in Natural Language Processing*, Barry G.T. Lowden, (ed.) University of Essex, Colchester, 8–23.

826. Knapp, Victor. 1982. Legal thesauri. In *Deontic Logic, Computational Linguistics and Legal Information Systems*, Antonio A. Martino, (ed.) North-Holland, Amsterdam, 267–290.

827. Knorz, G. 1982. Recognition of abstract objects - a decision theory approach within natural language processing. In *COLING-82*, 161–166.

828. Kobsa, Alfred. 1984. Three steps in constructing mutual belief models from user assertions. In *ECAI-84*, 423–426.

829. Kobsa, Alfred, Jürgen Allgayer, Carola Reddig, Norbert Reithinger, Dagmar Schmauks, Karin Harbusch and Wolfgang Wahlster. 1986. Combining deictic gestures and natural language for referent identification. In *COLING-86*, 356–361.

830. Koch, Dietrich. 1984. German language questioning for relational databases. In *Artificial Intelligence and Information-Control Systems of Robots*, Ivan Plander, (ed.) North-Holland, Amsterdam, 221–224.

831. Koch, Gregers. 1986. Computational linguistics and mathematical logic from a computer science point of view. In *Papers from the Fifth Scandinavian Conference of Computational Linguistics*, Fred Karlsson, (ed.) University of Helsinki, Helsinki, 131–142.

832. Koit, Mare, S. Litvak, H. Oim, T. Roosmaa and Madis Saluveer. 1983. Local and global structures in discourse understanding. In *ACL Proceedings, First European Conference*, 152–154.

833. Koit, Mare and Madis Saluveer. 1986. Generating natural language text in a dialog system. In *COLING-86*, 576–580.

834. Koktova, Eva. 1983. Towards the semantics of sentence adverbials. In *ACL Proceedings, First European Conference*, 74–80.

835. Koktova, Eva. 1985. Towards a new type of morphemic analysis. In *ACL Proceedings, Second European Conference*, 179–186.

836. Koktova, Eva. 1986. Sentence adverbials in a system of question answering without a prearranged data base. In *COLING-86*, 68–73.

837. Konolige, Kurt. 1980. Capturing linguistic generalizations with metarules in an annotated phrase-structure grammar. In *ACL Proceedings, 18th Annual Meeting*, 43–48.

838. Kononenko, I.S. and E.L Pershina. 1983. An experiment on synthesis of Russian parametric constructions. In *ACL Proceedings, First European Conference*, 129–132.

839. Kononenko, I.S. 1986. Speech acts of assertion in cooperative informational dialogue. In *COLING-86*, 515–519.

840. Kornai, Andras. 1985. Natural languages and the Chomsky hierarchy. In *ACL Proceedings, Second European Conference*, 1–7.

841. Koskenniemi, Kimmo. 1983. Two-level model for morphological analysis. In *IJCAI-83*, 683–685.

842. Koskenniemi, Kimmo. 1983. *Two-level Morphology: a general computational model for word-form recognition and production.* University of Helsinki, Helsinki.

843. Koskenniemi, Kimmo. 1984. A general computational model for word-form recognition and production. In *COLING-84*, 178–181.

844. Koskenniemi, Kimmo. 1985. A general two-level computational model for word-form recognition and production. In *Computational Morphosyntax: Report on Research 1981–1984*, Fred Karlsson, (ed.) University of Helsinki, Helsinki, 1–18.

845. Koskenniemi, Kimmo. 1985. An application of the two-level model to Finnish. In *Computational Morphosyntax: Report on Research 1981–1984*, Fred Karlsson, (ed.) University of Helsinki, Helsinki, 19–42.

846. Koskenniemi, Kimmo. 1985. A system for generating Finnish inflected word-forms. In *Computational Morphosyntax: Report on Research 1981–1984*, Fred Karlsson, (ed.) University of Helsinki, Helsinki, 63–80.

847. Koskenniemi, Kimmo. 1985. FINSTEMS: a module for information retrieval. In *Computational Morphosyntax: Report on Research 1981–1984*, Fred Karlsson, (ed.) University of Helsinki, Helsinki, 81–92.

848. Koskenniemi, Kimmo. 1986. Compilation of automata from morphological two-level rules. In *Papers from the Fifth Scandinavian Conference of Computational Linguistics*, Fred Karlsson, (ed.) University of Helsinki, Helsinki, 143–150.

849. Kosy, Donald W. 1986. Parsing conjunctions deterministically. In *ACL Proceedings, 24th Annual Meeting*, 78–84.

850. Kotsanis, Yannis and Yanis Maistros. 1985. "Lexi Fanis" : a lexical analyzer of modern Greek. In *ACL Proceedings, Second European Conference*, 154–158.

851. Krauwer, Steven and Louis des Tombe. 1984. Transfer in a multilingual MT system. In *COLING-84*, 464–467.

852. Kroch, Anthony S. 1982. On the linguistic character of nonstandard input. In *ACL Proceedings, 20th Annual Meeting*, 161–163.

853. Kroch, Anthony S. 1987. Limits on the human sentence generator. In *TINLAP-3*, 192–199.

854. Kronfeld, Amichai. 1986. Donellan's distinction and a computational model of reference. In *ACL Proceedings, 24th Annual Meeting*, 186–191.

855. Kronfeld, Amichai. 1987. Goals of referring acts. In *TINLAP-3*, 143–149.

856. Krulee, Gilbert K. 1986. Two-level processing systems. In *CLS 22, Part 1, Papers from the General Session*, Anne M. Farley, Peter T. Farley and Karl-Erik McCullough, (eds.) Chicago Linguistic Society, Chicago, 344–360.

857. Ksiezyk, Tomasz, Ralph Grishman and John Sterling. 1987. An equipment model and its role in the interpretation of noun phrases. *IJCAI-87* 2, 692–695.

858. Kučera, Henry. 1980. Computational analysis of predicational structures in English. In *COLING-80*, 32–37.

859. Kučera, Henry. 1982. Markedness and frequency: a computational analysis. In *COLING-82*, 167–173.

860. Kudo, Ikuo and Hirosato Nomura. 1986. Lexical-functional transfer: a transfer framework in a machine translation system based on LFG. In *COLING-86*, 112–114.

861. Kuhlen, Rainer. 1984. An international Delphi poll on future trends in information linguistics. In *COLING-84*, 540–545.

862. Kuhns, Robert J. 1986. A PROLOG implementation of government-binding theory. In *COLING-86*, 546–550.

863. Kukich, Karen. 1983. Knowledge-based report generation: a technique for automatically generating natural language reports from databases. In *Proceedings of the ACM SIGIR conference on research and development in information retrieval*, Bethesda, 307–344.

864. Kukich, Karen. 1983. Design and implementation of a knowledge-based report generator. In *ACL Proceedings, 21st Annual Meeting*, 145–150.

865. Kukich, Karen. 1985. Link-dependent message generation in XSEL. In *ACL Proceedings, 23rd Annual Meeting*, 228–237.

866. Kuno, Susumu and A.G Oettinger. 1986 (1962). Multiple path syntactic analyzer. In *Readings in Natural Language Processing*, Barbara J. Grosz, Karen Sparck-Jones and Bonnie Lynn Webber, (eds.) Morgan Kaufmann, Los Altos, 17–23.

867. Kunze, Jürgen. 1986. Temporal relations in texts and time logical inferences. In *COLING-86*, 350–352.

868. Kurtzman, Howard S. 1984. Ambiguity resolution in the human syntactic parser: an experimental study. In *COLING-84*, 481–485.

869. Kusanagi, Yutaka. 1980. A model of natural language processing of time-related expressions. In *COLING-80*, 101–107.

870. Kusanagi, Yutaka. 1984. Some linguistic aspects for automatic text understanding. In *COLING-84*, 409–412.

871. Kümmel, Peter. 1980. Content guided answer search system for natural languages. In *COLING-80*, 559–561.

872. Kwasny, Stan C. and Norman K Sondheimer. 1981. Relaxation theories for parsing ill-formed input. *American Journal of Computational Linguistics* 7:2, 99–108.

873. Kwasny, Stan C. 1982. Ill-formed and non-standard language problems. In *ACL Proceedings, 20th Annual Meeting*, 164–166.

874. Lakoff, George. 1987. Position paper on metaphor. In *TINLAP-3*, 173–176.

875. Lancel, Jean-Marie, Francois Rousselot and Nathalie Simonin. 1986. A grammar used for parsing and generation. In *COLING-86*, 536–539.

876. Landsbergen, S.P. Jan. 1980. Adaptation of Montague grammar to the requirements of question-answering. In *COLING-80*, 211–212.

877. Landsbergen, S.P. Jan. 1981. Adaptation of Montague grammar to the requirements of parsing. In *Formal Methods in the Study of Language*, J.A.G. Groenendijk, T.M.V. Janssen and M.B.J. Stokhof, (eds.) Mathematisch Centrum, Amsterdam, 399–419.

878. Landsbergen, S.P. Jan. 1982. Machine translation based on logically isomorphic Montague grammars. In *COLING-82*, 175–181.

879. Landsbergen, S.P. Jan. 1985. Montague grammar and machine translation. In *Proceedings of the Alvey/ICL Workshop on Linguistic Theory and Computer Applications*, Peter Whitelock, Harold Somers, Paul Bennett, Rod L. Johnson and Mary McGee Wood, (eds.) CCL/UMIST, Manchester, 76–94.

880. Langendoen, D. Terence and Yedidyah Langsam. 1984. The representation of constituent structures for finite-state parsing. In *COLING-84*, 24–27.

881. Langendoen, D. Terence and Paul M Postal. 1984. Comments on Pullum's criticisms. *Computational Linguistics* 10:3–4, 187–188.

882. Langley, Pat. 1980. A production system model of first language acquisition. In *COLING-80*, 183–189.

883. Langley, Pat. 1982. A model of early syntactic development. In *ACL Proceedings, 20th Annual Meeting*, 145–151.

884. LaPolla, Mark V. 1986. The role of inversion and PP-fronting in relating discourse-elements: some implications for cognitive and computational models of natural language processing. In *COLING-86*, 168–173.

885. Laubsch, J.H., Dietmar F. Rösner and Kenji Hanakata. 1984. Language generation from conceptual structure: synthesis of German in a Japanese/German MT project. In *COLING-84*, 491–494.

886. Laubsch, Joachim H. and Dietmar F Rösner. 1980. Active schemata and their role in semantic parsing. In *COLING-80*, 364–367.

887. Laurian, Anne-Marie. 1984. Machine translation: what type of post-editing on what type of documents for what type of users. In *COLING-84*, 236–238.

888. Lawson, Veronica. 1986. As the generations pass. *Computers and Translation* 1:1, 61.

889. Lawson, Veronica. 1986. The background to practical machine translation. *Computers and Translation* 1:2, 109–112.

890. Lebowitz, Michael. 1980. Language and memory: generalization as a part of understanding. In *AAAI-80*, 324–326.

891. Lebowitz, Michael. 1981. The nature of generalization in understanding. *IJCAI-81* 1, 348–353.

892. Lebowitz, Michael. 1981. Cancelled due to lack of interest. *IJCAI-81* 1, 13–15.

893. Lebowitz, Michael. 1983. Generalization from natural language text. *Cognitive Science* 7:1, 1–40.

894. Lebowitz, Michael. 1983. RESEARCHER: an overview. In *AAAI-83*, 232–235.

895. Lebowitz, Michael. 1984. Using memory in text understanding. In *ECAI-84*, 369–378.

896. Lebowitz, Michael. 1985. RESEARCHER: an experimental intelligent information system. *IJCAI-85* 2, 858–862.

897. Lebowitz, Michael. 1985. Using memory in text understanding. In *Advances in Artificial Intelligence*, Tim O'Shea, (ed.) North-Holland, Amsterdam, 159–168.

898. Lee, Lin-shan, Chiu-yu Tseng, K.J. Chen and James Huang. 1987. The preliminary results of a Mandarin dictation machine based upon Chinese natural language analysis. *IJCAI-87* 2, 619–621.

899. Lehmann, Winfred P. 1982. My term. In *ACL Proceedings, 20th Annual Meeting*, 97.

900. Lehnert, Wendy G. 1986 (1977). A conceptual theory of question answering. In *Readings in Natural Language Processing*, Barbara J. Grosz, Karen Sparck-Jones and Bonnie Lynn Webber, (eds.) Morgan Kaufmann, Los Altos, 651–657.

901. Lehnert, Wendy G. 1980. Narrative text summarization. In *AAAI-80*, 337–339.

902. Lehnert, Wendy G. 1980. Question answering in natural language processing. In *Natural Language Question Answering Systems*, Leonard Bolc, (ed.) Hanser, Munich, 9–71.

903. Lehnert, Wendy G. 1981. Plot units and narrative summarization. *Cognitive Science* 5:4, 293–332.

904. Lehnert, Wendy G. 1981. A computational theory of human question answering. In *Elements of Discourse Understanding*, Aravind K. Joshi, Bonnie Lynn Webber and Ivan Sag, (eds.) Cambridge University Press, Cambridge, 145–176.

905. Lehnert, Wendy G., John B. Black and Brian J Reister. 1981. Summarizing narratives. *IJCAI-81* 1, 184–189.

906. Lehnert, Wendy G. 1982. Plot units: a narrative summarization strategy. In *Strategies for Natural Language Processing*, Wendy G. Lehnert and Martin H. Ringle, (eds.) Erlbaum, Hillsdale, 375–414.

907. Lehnert, Wendy G. and Martin H. Ringle, (eds.) 1982. *Strategies for Natural Language Processing*. Erlbaum, Hillsdale.

908. Lehnert, Wendy G. 1983. Narrative complexity based on summarization algorithms. In *IJCAI-83*, 713–716.

909. Lehnert, Wendy G., Michael G. Dyer, Philip N. Johnson, C.J. Yang and S Harley. 1983. BORIS - an experiment in in-depth understanding of narratives. *Artificial Intelligence* 20:1, 15–62.

910. Lehnert, Wendy G. and Steven P Shwartz. 1983. Explorer: a natural language processing system for oil exploration. In *ACL Proceedings, Conference on Applied Natural Language Processing*, 69–72.

911. Lehnert, Wendy G. 1984. Narrative complexity based on summarization algorithms. In *Computational Models of Natural Language Processing*, Bruno G. Bara and Giovanni Guida, (eds.) North-Holland, Amsterdam, 247–259.

912. Lehnert, Wendy G. 1987. Possible implications of connectionism. In *TINLAP-3*, 78–83.

913. Lehtola, Aarno, Harri Jäppinen and Esa Nelimarkka. 1985. Language-based environment for natural language parsing. In *ACL Proceedings, Second European Conference*, 98–106.

914. Lehtola, Aarno. 1986. DPL - a computational method for describing grammars and modelling parsers. In *Papers from the Fifth Scandinavian Conference of Computational Linguistics*, Fred Karlsson, (ed.) University of Helsinki, Helsinki, 151–160.

915. Leonard, Rosemary. 1984. *The Interpretation of English Noun Sequences on the Computer*. North-Holland, Amsterdam.

916. Lepage, Yves. 1986. A language for transcriptions. In *COLING-86*, 402–404.

917. Lesmo, Leonardo and Pietro Torasso. 1983. A flexible natural language parser based on a two-level representation of syntax. In *ACL Proceedings, First European Conference*, 114–121.

918. Lesmo, Leonardo and Pietro Torasso. 1984. Interpreting syntactically ill-formed sentences. In *COLING-84*, 534–539.

919. Lesmo, Leonardo and Pietro Torasso. 1985. Weighted interaction of syntax and semantics in natural language analysis. *IJCAI-85* 2, 772–778.

920. Lesmo, Leonardo and Pietro Torasso. 1985. Analysis of conjunctions in a rule-based parser. In *ACL Proceedings, 23rd Annual Meeting*, 180–187.

921. Lespérance, Yves. 1986. Toward a computational interpretation of situation semantics. *Computational Intelligence* 2:1, 9–27.

922. Léon, J., D. Memmi, M. Ornato, J. Pomian and Gian Piero Zarri. 1982. Conversion of a French surface expression into its semantic representation according to the RESEDA metalanguage. In *COLING-82*, 183–189.

923. Li, Ping-Yang, Martha Evens and Daniel Hier. 1986. Generating medical case reports with the linguistic string parser. *AAAI-86* 2, 1069–1073.

924. Liberman, Mark. 1986. Questions about connectionist models of natural language. In *ACL Proceedings, 24th Annual Meeting*, 181–183.

925. Lin, Long Ji, Lin-Shan Lee, James Huang and K.J Chen. 1986. A Chinese natural language processing system based upon the theory of empty categories. *AAAI-86* 2, 1059–1062.

926. Linde, Charlotte and J.A Gougen. 1980. On the independence of discourse structure and semantic domain. In *ACL Proceedings, 18th Annual Meeting*, 35–37.

927. Litkowski, Kenneth C. 1980. Requirements of text processing lexicons. In *ACL Proceedings, 18th Annual Meeting*, 153–154.

928. Litman, Diane J. and James F Allen. 1984. A plan recognition model for clarification subdialogues. In *COLING-84*, 302–311.

929. Litman, Diane J. 1986. Linguistic coherence: a plan-based alternative. In *ACL Proceedings, 24th Annual Meeting*, 215–223.

930. Litman, Diane J. 1986. Understanding plan ellipsis. *AAAI-86* 1, 619–624.

931. Lockman, Abe. 1980. Semantics and parts of speech. In *Proceedings of the Third Biennial Conference of the Canadian Society for Computational Studies of Intelligence (3rd Canadian Conference on AI)*, 129–130.

932. Lockman, Abe and David Klappholz. 1983. The control of inferencing in natural language understanding. *Computers and Mathematics with Applications* 9:1, 59–70.

933. Longuet-Higgins, Christopher. 1981. Procedural theories of linguistic performance. *Philosophical Transactions of the Royal Society, Series B* 295:1077, 297–304.

934. Loong-Cheong, Tong. 1986. English-Malay translation system: a laboratory prototype. In *COLING-86*, 639–642.

935. Lopes, Gabriel Pereira. 1984. Transforming English interfaces to other natural languages: an experiment with Portuguese. In *COLING-84*, 8–10.

936. Lopes, Gabriel Pereira and Rosa Maria Viccari. 1984. An intelligent monitor interaction in Portugese language. In *ECAI-84*, 109–113.

937. Lopes, Gabriel Pereira. 1985. Implementing Dialogues in a knowledge information system. In *Proceedings of an International Workshop on Natural Language Understanding and Logic Programming, University of Rennes.*

938. Lozinskii, E.L. and Sergei Nirenburg. 1982. Parallel processing of natural language. In *ECAI-82*, 216–221.

939. Lubonski, Pawel. 1985. Natural language interface for a Polish railway expert system. In *Natural Language Understanding and Logic Programming*, Veronica Dahl and Patrick Saint-Dizier, (eds.) North-Holland, Amsterdam, 21–31.

940. Luckhardt, Heinz-Dirk. 1986. Controlled active procedures as a tool for linguistic engineering. In *COLING-86*, 464–469.

941. Luctkens, E. and P.H Fermont. 1986. A prototype machine translation based on extracts from data processing manuals. In *COLING-86*, 643–645.

942. Lun, S. 1983. A two-level morphological analysis of French. *Texas Linguistic Forum* 22, 271–278.

943. Luria, Marc. 1982. Dividing up the question answering process. In *AAAI-82*, 71–74.

944. Luria, Marc. 1987. Expressing concern. In *ACL Proceedings, 25th Annual Meeting*, 221–227.

945. Lytinen, Steven L. 1984. Frame selection in parsing. In *AAAI-84*, 222–225.

946. Lytinen, Steven L. 1986. Dynamically combining syntax and semantics in natural language processing. *AAAI-86* 1, 574–578.

947. Lytinen, Steven L. and Anatole V Gershman. 1986. ATRANS: automatic processing of money transfer messages. *AAAI-86* 2, 1089–1093.

948. Lytinen, Steven L. 1987. Integrating syntax and semantics. In *Machine Translation: Theoretical and Methodological Issues*, Sergei Nirenberg, (ed.) Cambridge University Press, Cambridge, 302–316.

949. Maier, David and Sharon C Salveter. 1982. Supporting natural language updates in database systems. In *ECAI-82*, 244–249.

950. Main, Michael G. and David B Benson. 1983. Denotational semantics for 'natural' language question-answering programs. *American Journal of Computational Linguistics* 9:1, 11–21.

951. Makino, Hiroshi and Makoto Kizawa. 1980. An automatic translation system of non-segmented Kana sentences into Kanji-Kana sentences. In *COLING-80*, 295–302.

952. Malkovsky, M.G. 1982. TULIPS-2 - natural language learning system. In *COLING-82*, 191–193.

953. Mallery, John C. 1985. Universality and individuality: the interaction of noun phrase determiners in copular clauses. In *ACL Proceedings, 23rd Annual Meeting*, 35–42.

954. Manaster-Ramer, Alexis. 1986. Copying in natural languages, context-freeness, and queue grammars. In *ACL Proceedings, 24th Annual Meeting*, 85–89.

955. Manaster-Ramer, Alexis. 1987. Subject-verb agreement in respective coordinations and context freeness. *Computational Linguistics* 13:1–2, 64–65.

956. Mann, William C. 1981. Selective planning of interface evaluations. In *ACL Proceedings, 19th Annual Meeting*, 33–34.

957. Mann, William C. 1981. Two discourse generators. In *ACL Proceedings, 19th Annual Meeting*, 43–47.

958. Mann, William C. and James A Moore. 1981. Computer generation of multiparagraph English text. *American Journal of Computational Linguistics* 7:1, 17–29.

959. Mann, William C. 1982. The anatomy of a systemic choice. In *COLING-82*, 195–200.

960. Mann, William C. 1982. Text generation. *American Journal of Computational Linguistics* 8:2, 62–69.

961. Mann, William C. 1983. Inquiry semantics: a functional semantics of natural language grammar. In *ACL Proceedings, First European Conference*, 165–174.

962. Mann, William C. 1983. An overview of the Nigel text generation grammar. In *ACL Proceedings, 21st Annual Meeting*, 79–84.

963. Mann, William C. 1983. An overview of the Penman text generation system. In *AAAI-83*, 261–265.

964. Mann, William C. 1984. Discourse structures for text generation. In *COLING-84*, 367–377.

965. Mann, William C. 1987. What is special about natural language generation research ?. In *TINLAP-3*, 206–210.

966. Marburger, Heinz, Bernd Neumann and Hans-Joachim Novak. 1981. Natural language dialogue about moving objects in an automatically analyzed traffic scene. *IJCAI-81* 1, 49–51.

967. Marburger, Heinz and Wolfgang Wahlster. 1983. Case role filling as a side effect of visual search. In *ACL Proceedings, First European Conference*, 189–195.

968. Marcus, Claudia. 1986. *Prolog Programming: Applications for Database Systems, Expert Systems and Natural Language Systems.* Addison-Wesley, Reading, Ma..

969. Marcus, Mitchell P. 1986 (1978). A computational account of some constraints on language. In *Readings in Natural Language Processing*, Barbara J. Grosz, Karen Sparck-Jones and Bonnie Lynn Webber, (eds.) Morgan Kaufmann, Los Altos, 89–99.

970. Marcus, Mitchell P. 1980. *A Theory of Syntactic Recognition for Natural Language*. MIT Press, Cambridge, Ma..

971. Marcus, Mitchell P. 1981. A computational account of some constraints on language. In *Elements of Discourse Understanding*, Aravind K. Joshi, Bonnie Lynn Webber and Ivan Sag, (eds.) Cambridge University Press, Cambridge, 177–200.

972. Marcus, Mitchell P. 1982. Building non-normative systems - the search for robustness: an overview. In *ACL Proceedings, 20th Annual Meeting*, 152.

973. Marcus, Mitchell P., Donald Hindle and Margaret Fleck. 1983. D-theory: talking about talking about trees. In *ACL Proceedings, 21st Annual Meeting*, 129–136.

974. Marcus, Mitchell P. 1985. Deterministic parsing and description theory. In *Proceedings of the Alvey/ICL Workshop on Linguistic Theory and Computer Applications*, Peter Whitelock, Harold Somers, Paul Bennett, Rod L. Johnson and Mary McGee Wood, (eds.) CCL/UMIST, Manchester, 49–75.

975. Marcus, Mitchell P. 1987. Generation systems should choose their words. In *TINLAP-3*, 211–214.

976. Mark, William. 1985. Special purpose reasoning in the Consul system. In *Theoretiçal Approaches to Natural Language Understanding, a Workshop at Halifax, Nova Scotia*, 14–20.

977. Markowitz, Judith, Thomas E. Ahlswede and Martha Evens. 1986. Semantically significant patterns in dictionary definitions. In *ACL Proceedings, 24th Annual Meeting*, 112–119.

978. Marsh, Elaine and Naomi Sager. 1982. Analysis and processing of compact text. In *COLING-82*, 201–206.

979. Marsh, Elaine. 1983. Utilizing domain-specific information for processing compact text. In *ACL Proceedings, Conference on Applied Natural Language Processing*, 99–103.

980. Marsh, Elaine. 1984. A computational analysis of complex noun phrases in navy messages. In *COLING-84*, 505–508.

981. Marsh, Elaine, Henry Hamburger and Ralph Grishman. 1984. A production rule system for message summarization. In *AAAI-84*, 243–246.

982. Martin, Paul, Douglas E. Appelt and Fernando C.N Pereira. 1986 (1983). Transportability and generality in natural language interface system. In *Readings in Natural Language Processing*, Barbara J. Grosz, Karen Sparck-Jones and Bonnie Lynn Webber, (eds.) Morgan Kaufmann, Los Altos, 585–593.

983. Martin, Paul, Douglas E. Appelt and Fernando C.N Pereira. 1983. Transportability and generality in a natural language interface system. In *IJCAI-83*, 573–581.

984. Martin, William A. 1980. Parsing. In *ACL Proceedings, 18th Annual Meeting*, 91–93.

985. Martin, William A. 1981. Roles, co-descriptors, and the formal representation of quantified English expressions. *American Journal of Computational Linguistics* 7:3, 137–147.

986. Martino, Antonio A., (ed.) 1982. *Deontic Logic, Computational Linguistics and Legal Information Systems*. North-Holland, Amsterdam.

987. Martins, Gary. 1983. Machine translation. In *ACL Proceedings, Conference on Applied Natural Language Processing*, 148.

988. Maruyama, F. and A Yonezawa. 1984. A PROLOG-based natural language front-end system. *New Generation Computing* 2, 00–00.

989. Mathiessen, Christian M.I.M. 1981. A grammar and a lexicon for a text-production system. In *ACL Proceedings, 19th Annual Meeting*, 49–55.

990. Mathiessen, Christian M.I.M. 1983. Systemic grammar in computation: the Nigel case. In *ACL Proceedings, First European Conference*, 155–164.

991. Mathieu, Yvette and Paul Sabatier. 1986. INTERFACILE: linguistic coverage and query reformulation. In *COLING-86*, 46–49.

992. Matsumoto, Yuji. 1981. Software implementation of Montague Grammar and related problems. In *Formal Approaches to Natural Language*, Shogo Iguchi, (ed.) Kyoto Working Group of Montague Grammar, Kyoto, 148–158.

993. Matsumoto, Yuji, Hozumi Tanaka, H. Hirakawa, Hideo Miyoshi and Hideki Yasukawa. 1983. BUP: a bottom-up parser embedded in PROLOG. *New Generation Computing* 1, 145–158.

994. Matsumoto, Yuji, Masaki Kiyono and Hozumi Tanaka. 1985. Facilities of the BUP parsing system. In *Natural Language Understanding and Logic Programming*, Veronica Dahl and Patrick Saint-Dizier, (eds.) North-Holland, Amsterdam, 97–106.

995. Matsumoto, Yuji. 1986. A parallel parsing system for natural language analysis. In *Proceedings of the Third International Conference on Logic Programming*, Ehud Shapiro, (ed.) Springer, Berlin, 396–409.

996. Matsumoto, Yuji, Hozumi Tanaka and Masaki Kiyono. 1986. BUP: A bottom-up logic parsing system for natural languages. In *Logic Programming and its Applications (Volume 2)*, Michel van Caneg ham and David H.D. Warren, (eds.) Ablex, Norwood, New Jersey, 00–00.

997. Matsumoto, Yuji and Ryoichi Sugimura. 1987. A parsing system based on logic programming. *IJCAI-87* 2, 671–674.

998. Mauldin, Michael L. 1984. Semantic rule based text generation. In *COLING-84*, 378–380.

999. Maxwell, Michael. 1985. On double slash categories in GPSG. In *Theoretical Approaches to Natural Language Understanding, a Workshop at Halifax, Nova Scotia*, 89–97.

1000. Mays, Eric. 1980. Failures in natural language systems: applications to data base query systems. In *AAAI-80*, 327–330.

1001. Mays, Eric. 1980. Correcting misconceptions about data base structures. In *Proceedings of the Third Biennial Conference of the Canadian Society for Computational Studies of Intelligence (3rd Canadian Conference on AI)*, 123–128.

1002. Mays, Eric, Sitaram Lanka, Aravind K. Joshi and Bonnie Lynn Webber. 1981. Natural language interaction with dynamic knowledge bases: monitoring as response. *IJCAI-81* 1, 61–63.

1003. Mays, Eric, Aravind K. Joshi and Bonnie Lynn Webber. 1982. Taking the initiative in natural language data base interactions: monitoring as response. In *ECAI-82*, 255–256.

1004. Mays, Eric. 1983. A modal temporal logic for reasoning about change. In *ACL Proceedings, 21st Annual Meeting*, 38–43.

1005. Mays, Eric. 1985. Some conditions on providing a class of extended responses. In *Theoretical Approaches to Natural Language Understanding, a Workshop at Halifax, Nova Scotia*, 21–30.

1006. Mazlack, L.J. and R.A Feinauer. 1982. Surface analysis of queries directed toward a database. In *COLING-82*, 207–213.

1007. Mândutianu, Sanda. 1984. ROUND-S: an experiment with knowledge driven semantics in natural language understanding. In *Artificial Intelligence and Information-Control Systems of Robots*, Ivan Plander, (ed.) North-Holland, Amsterdam, 233–236.

1008. McCalla, Gordon I. 1983. An approach to the organization of knowledge and its use in natural language recall tasks. *Computers and Mathematics with Applications* 9:1, 201–214.

1009. McClelland, James L. 1986. The programmable blackboard model of reading. In *Parallel Distributed Processing*, James L. McClelland, David E. Rumelhart and the PDP Research Group, (eds.) vol. 2, MIT Press, Cambridge, Ma., 122–169.

1010. McClelland, James L. and A.H Kawamoto. 1986. Mechanisms of sentence processing: assigning roles to constituents of sentences. In *Parallel Distributed Processing*, James L. McClelland, David E. Rumelhart and the PDP Research Group, (eds.) vol. 2, MIT Press, Cambridge, Ma., 272–325.

1011. McClelland, James L. 1987. Parallel distributed processing and role assignment constraints. In *TINLAP-3*, 73–77.

1012. McCord, Michael C. 1980. Slot grammars. *American Journal of Computational Linguistics* 6:1, 31–43.

1013. McCord, Michael C. 1982. Using slots and modifiers in logic grammars for natural language. *Artificial Intelligence* 18:3, 327–368.

1014. McCord, Michael C. 1985. Modular logic grammars. In *ACL Proceedings, 23rd Annual Meeting*, 104–117.

1015. McCord, Michael C. 1986. Design of a PROLOG-based machine translation system. In *Proceedings of the Third International Conference on Logic Programming*, Ehud Shapiro, (ed.) Springer, Berlin, 350–374.

1016. McCord, Michael C. 1986. Focalizers, the scoping problem, and semantic interpretation rules in logic grammars. In *Logic Programming and its Applications (Volume 2)*, Michel van Canefham and David H.D. Warren, (eds.) Ablex, Norwood, New Jersey, 00–00.

1017. McCord, Michael C. 1987. Natural language processing in Prolog. In *Knowledge Systems and Prolog*, Adrian Walker, (ed.) Addison-Wesley, Reading, Ma., 291–402.

1018. McCoy, Kathleen F. 1082. Augmenting a database knowledge representation for natural language generation. In *ACL Proceedings, 20th Annual Meeting*, 121–128.

1019. McCoy, Kathleen F. 1984. Correcting object-related misconceptions: how should the system respond?. In *COLING-84*, 444–447.

1020. McCoy, Kathleen F. 1985. The role of perspective in responding to property misconceptions. *IJCAI-85* 2, 791–793.

1021. McCoy, Kathleen F. 1986. The ROMPER system: responding to object-related misconceptions using perspective. In *ACL Proceedings, 24th Annual Meeting*, 97–105.

1022. McDermott, Drew. 1986 (1978). Tarskian semantics, or no notation without denotation. In *Readings in Natural Language Processing*, Barbara J. Grosz, Karen Sparck-Jones and Bonnie Lynn Webber, (eds.) Morgan Kaufmann, Los Altos, 167–169.

1023. McDonald, David B. 1981. Compound: a program that understands noun compounds. *IJCAI-81* 2, 1061.

1024. McDonald, David D. 1986 (1983). Description directed control: its implications for natural language generation. In *Readings in Natural Language Processing*, Barbara J. Grosz, Karen Sparck-Jones and Bonnie Lynn Webber, (eds.) Morgan Kaufmann, Los Altos, 519–537.

1025. McDonald, David D. 1980. A linear-time model of language production: some psycholinguistic implications. In *ACL Proceedings, 18th Annual Meeting*, 55–57.

1026. McDonald, David D. 1980. The role of discourse structure in language production. In *Proceedings of the Third Biennial Conference of the Canadian Society for Computational Studies of Intelligence (3rd Canadian Conference on AI)*, 143–150.

1027. McDonald, David D. 1981. Language production: the source of the dictionary. In *ACL Proceedings, 19th Annual Meeting*, 57–62.

1028. McDonald, David D. 1981. MUMBLE: a flexible system for language production. *IJCAI-81* 2, 1062.

1029. McDonald, David D. and E. Jeffrey Conklin. 1982. Salience as a simplifying metaphor for natural language generation. In *AAAI-82*, 75–78.

1030. McDonald, David D. 1983. Description directed control: its implications for natural language generation. *Computers and Mathematics with Applications* 9:1, 111–129.

1031. McDonald, David D. 1983. Natural language generation as a computational problem: an introduction. In *Computational Models of Discourse*, Michael Brady and Robert C. Berwick, (eds.) MIT Press, Cambridge, Ma., 109–265.

1032. McDonald, David D. and James D Pustejovsky. 1985. A computational theory of prose style for natural language generation. In *ACL Proceedings, Second European Conference*, 187–193.

1033. McDonald, David D. and James D Pustejovsky. 1985. Description-directed natural language generation. *IJCAI-85* 2, 799–805.

1034. McDonald, David D. and James D Pustejovsky. 1985. TAGs as a grammatical formalism for generation. In *ACL Proceedings, 23rd Annual Meeting*, 94–103.

1035. McDonald, David D. 1987. Natural language generation: complexities and techniques. In *Machine Translation: Theoretical and Methodological Issues*, Sergei Nirenberg, (ed.) Cambridge University Press, Cambridge, 192–224.

1036. McDonald, David D. 1987. No better, but no worse, than people. In *TINLAP-3*, 200–205.

1037. McGuire, Rod, Lawrence Birnbaum and Margot Flowers. 1981. Opportunistic processing in arguments. *IJCAI-81* 1, 58–60.

1038. McKeown, Kathleen R. 1986 (1985). Discourse strategies for generating natural language text. In *Readings in Natural Language Processing*, Barbara J. Grosz, Karen Sparck-Jones and Bonnie Lynn Webber, (eds.) Morgan Kaufmann, Los Altos, 479–499.

1039. McKeown, Kathleen R. 1980. Generating relevant explanations: natural language responses to questions about database structure. In *AAAI-80*, 306–309.

1040. McKeown, Kathleen R. 1982. The TEXT system for natural language generation: an overview. In *ACL Proceedings, 20th Annual Meeting*, 113–120.

1041. McKeown, Kathleen R. 1983. Focus constraints on language generation. In *IJCAI-83*, 582–587.

1042. McKeown, Kathleen R. 1983. Recursion in TEXT and its use in language generation. In *AAAI-83*, 270–273.

1043. McKeown, Kathleen R. 1983. Paraphrasing questions using given and new information. *American Journal of Computational Linguistics* 9:1, 1–10.

1044. McKeown, Kathleen R. 1984. Using focus to constrain language generation. In *Computational Models of Natural Language Processing*, Bruno G. Bara and Giovanni Guida, (eds.) North-Holland, Amsterdam, 261–274.

1045. McKeown, Kathleen R. 1984. Natural language for expert systems: comparisons with database systems. In *COLING-84*, 190–193.

1046. McKeown, Kathleen R., Myron Wish and Kevin Matthews. 1985. Tailoring explanations for the user. *IJCAI-85* 2, 794–798.

1047. McKeown, Kathleen R. 1985. Discourse strategies for generating natural language text. *Artificial Intelligence* 27:1, 1–42.

1048. McKeown, Kathleen R. 1985. *Text Generation: Using Discourse Strategies and Focus Constraints to Generate Natural Language Text*. Cambridge University Press, Cambridge.

1049. McKeown, Kathleen R. and Cecile R Paris. 1987. Functional unification grammar revisited. In *ACL Proceedings, 25th Annual Meeting*, 97–103.

1050. McNaught, John. 1983. The generation of term definitions from an on-line terminological thesaurus. In *ACL Proceedings, First European Conference*, 90–95.

1051. McPeters, David L. and Alan L Tharp. 1983. Application of the Liberman-Prince stress rules to computer synthesized speech. In *ACL Proceedings, Conference on Applied Natural Language Processing*, 192–197.

1052. McTear, Michael. 1987. *The Articulate Computer*. Blackwell, Oxford.

1053. Meehan, James. 1981. TALE-SPIN. In *Inside Computer Understanding: Five Programs plus Miniatures*, Roger C. Schank and Christopher K. Riesbeck, (eds.) Erlbaum, Hillsdale, 197–226.

1054. Meehan, James. 1981. Micro TALE-SPIN. In *Inside Computer Understanding: Five Programs plus Miniatures*, Roger C. Schank and Christopher K. Riesbeck, (eds.) Erlbaum, Hillsdale, 227–258.

1055. Melby, Alan K., Melvin R. Smith and Jill Peterson. 1980. ITS: interactive translation system. In *COLING-80*, 424–429.

1056. Melby, Alan K. 1982. Multi-level translation aids in a distributed system. In *COLING-82*, 215–220.

1057. Melby, Alan K. 1983. Computer assisted translation systems: the standard design and a multi-level design. In *ACL Proceedings, Conference on Applied Natural Language Processing*, 174–177.

1058. Melby, Alan K. 1985. Machine translation vs. translator aids: a false dichotomy. In *Humans and Machines: 4th Delaware Symposium on Language Studies*, Stephanie Williams, (ed.) Ablex, Norwood, 45–53.

1059. Melby, Alan K. 1986. Lexical transfer: a missing element in linguistic theories. In *COLING-86*, 104–106.

1060. Melby, Alan K. 1987. On human machine interaction in translation. In *Machine Translation: Theoretical and Methodological Issues*, Sergei Nirenberg, (ed.) Cambridge University Press, Cambridge, 145–154.

1061. Mellish, Christopher S. 1980. Some problems in early noun phrase interpretations. In *AISB-80*, 197–201.

1062. Mellish, Christopher S. 1983. Incremental semantic interpretation in a modular parsing system. In *Automatic Natural Language Parsing*, Karen Sparck-Jones and Yorick A. Wilks, (eds.) Ellis Horwood/Wiley, Chichester/New York, 148–155.

1063. Mellish, Christopher S. 1984. Introduction to the natural language processing subfield. In *ECAI-84*, 125.

1064. Mellish, Christopher S. 1984. Towards top-down generation of multi-paragraph text. In *ECAI-84*, 229.

1065. Mellish, Christopher S. 1985. *Computer Interpretation of Natural Language Descriptions*. Ellis Horwood/Wiley, Chichester/New York.

1066. Memmi, D. and J Mariani. 1982. ARBUS, a tool for developing application grammars. In *COLING-82*, 221–226.

1067. Menzel, Wolfgang. 1984. Data optimization in natural language based systems. In *Artificial Intelligence and Information-Control Systems of Robots*, Ivan Plander, (ed.) North-Holland, Amsterdam, 247–250.

1068. Mercer, Robert E. and Raymond Reiter. 1982. The representation of presuppositions using defaults. In *Proceedings of the 4th National Conference of the Canadian Society for Computational Studies of Intelligence, Saskatoon, Canada, May 17–19*, 103–107.

1069. Messick, Steven L. 1985. Language as a knowledge engineering tool. In *Theoretical Approaches to Natural Language Understanding, a Workshop at Halifax, Nova Scotia*, 133.

1070. Metzing, Dieter. 1980. ATNs used as a procedural dialog model. In *COLING-80*, 487–491.

1071. Meunier, Jean-Guy. 1980. Semantics for text processing. In *COLING-80*, 359–363.

1072. Meunier, Jean-Guy and F Lepage. 1983. Formal semantic and computer text processing, 1982. *Computers and Mathematics with Applications* 9:1, 83–95.

1073. Meyers, Amnon. 1985. VOX - an extensible natural language processor. *IJCAI-85* 2, 821–825.

1074. Michell, B. G., N.J. Belkin and D.G Kuehner. 1980. Representation of texts for information retrieval. In *ACL Proceedings, 18th Annual Meeting*, 147–148.

1075. Michiels, A., J. Mullenders and J Noël. 1980. Exploiting a large data base by LONGMAN. In *COLING-80*, 374–382.

1076. Michiels, A. and J.Noël. 1982. Approaches to thesaurus production. In *COLING-82*, 227–232.

1077. Mihailova, G. and G Gargov. 1984. A formal approach to verb semantics. In *Artificial Intelligence and Information-Control Systems of Robots*, Ivan Plander, (ed.) North-Holland, Amsterdam, 251–254.

1078. Miller, Dale A. and Gopalan Nadathur. 1986. Some uses of higher-order logic in computational linguistics. In *ACL Proceedings, 24th Annual Meeting*, 247–256.

1079. Miller, George A. and Donna M Kwilosz. 1981. Interactions of modality and negation in English. In *Elements of Discourse Understanding*, Aravind K. Joshi, Bonnie Lynn Webber and Ivan Sag, (eds.) Cambridge University Press, Cambridge, 201–216.

1080. Miller, George A. 1984. How to misread a dictionary. In *COLING-84*, 462.

1081. Miller, George A. 1985. Dictionaries of the mind. In *ACL Proceedings, 23rd Annual Meeting*, 305–314.

1082. Miller, Lance A. 1980. Project EPISTLE: a system for the automatic analysis of business correspondence. In *AAAI-80*, 280–282.

1083. Miller, Lance A. 1982. Natural language texts are not necessarily grammatical and unambiguous or even complete. In *ACL Proceedings, 20th Annual Meeting*, 167–168.

1084. Milne, Robert W. 1980. Parsing against lexical ambiguity. In *COLING-80*, 350–353.

1085. Milne, Robert W. 1980. Using determinism to predict garden paths. In *AISB-80*, 202–207.

1086. Milne, Robert W. 1982. An explanation for minimal attachment and right association. In *AAAI-82*, 88–90.

1087. Minker, Jack and Patricia B Powell. 1980. Answer and reason extraction, natural language and voice output for deductive data bases. In *Natural Language Based Computer Systems*, Leonard Bolc, (ed.) Hanser, Munich, 9–56.

1088. Minton, Steve, Philip J. Hayes and Jill Fain. 1985. Controlling search in flexible parsing. *IJCAI-85* 2, 785–787.

1089. Miyoshi, Hideo and Koichi Furukawa. 1985. Object-oriented parser in the logic programming language ESP. In *Natural Language Understanding and Logic Programming*, Veronica Dahl and Patrick Saint-Dizier, (eds.) North-Holland, Amsterdam, 107–119.

1090. Mizoguchi, F. and S Kondo. 1982. A software environment for developing natural language understanding system. In *COLING-82*, 233–238.

1091. Mizoguchi, Fumio and Akihiko Yamamoto. 1980. An approach to a semantic analysis of metaphor. In *COLING-80*, 136–143.

1092. Moens, Marc and Mark J Steedman. 1987. Temporal ontology in natural language. In *ACL Proceedings, 25th Annual Meeting*, 1–7.

1093. Moerdler, Galina Datskovsky, Kathleen R. McKeown and J. Robert Ensor. 1987. Building natural language interfaces for rule-based expert systems. *IJCAI-87* 2, 682–687.

1094. Momouchi, Yoshio. 1980. Control structures for actions in procedural texts and PT-charts. In *COLING-80*, 108–114.

1095. Montgomery, Christine A. 1982. Concept extraction. *American Journal of Computational Linguistics* 8:2, 70–73.

1096. Montgomery, Christine A. 1983 p55–61. Distinguishing fact from opinion and events from meta-events. In *ACL Proceedings, Conference on Applied Natural Language Processing*.

1097. Mooney, Raymond and Gerald F. DeJong. 1985. Learning schemata for natural language processing. *IJCAI-85* 1, 681–687.

1098. Moore, Robert C. 1986 (1981). Problems in logical form. In *Readings in Natural Language Processing*, Barbara J. Grosz, Karen Sparck-Jones and Bonnie Lynn Webber, (eds.) Morgan Kaufmann, Los Altos, 285–292.

1099. Moore, Robert C. 1981. Problems in logical form. In *ACL Proceedings, 19th Annual Meeting*, 117–124.

1100. Moore, Robert C. 1982. Natural-language access to databases - theoretical/technical issues. In *ACL Proceedings, 20th Annual Meeting*, 44–45.

1101. Moore, Robert C. and Graeme D Ritchie. 1986. *Natural Language Processing*. ECAI-86 tutorial volume, Brighton.

1102. Moore, Robert C. 1987. Properties and propositions. In *Proceedings of the Alvey Sponsored Workshop on Formal Semantics in Natural Language Processing*, Barry G.T. Lowden, (ed.) University of Essex, Colchester, 82.

1103. Moran, Douglas B. 1981. Presupposition and implicature in model-theoretic pragmatics. In *ACL Proceedings, 19th Annual Meeting*, 107–108.

1104. Moran, Douglas B. 1982. The representation of inconsistent information in a dynamic model-theoretic semantics. In *ACL Proceedings, 20th Annual Meeting*, 16–18.

1105. Morik, Katharina. 1983. Demand and requirements for natural language systems - results of an inquiry. In *IJCAI-83*, 647–649.

1106. Morik, Katharina. 1985. User modelling, dialog structure, and dialog strategy in Ham-Ans. In *ACL Proceedings, Second European Conference*, 268–273.

1107. Moshier, M. Drew and William C Rounds. 1987. On the succintness properties or unordered context-free grammars. In *ACL Proceedings, 25th Annual Meeting*, 112–116.

1108. Moyne, John A. 1985. *Understanding Language: Man or Machine*. Plenum, New York.

1109. Mudler, Joachim. 1983. A system for improving the recognition of fluently spoken German speech. In *IJCAI-83*, 633–636.

1110. Mueckstein, Eva-Marie M. 1983. Q-TRANS: Query translation into English. In *IJCAI-83*, 660–662.

1111. Mukai, Kuniaki and Hideki Yasukawa. 1985. Complex indeterminates in PROLOG and its application to discourse models. *New Generation Computing* 3, 441–466.

1112. Munch, Klaus H. 1986. Domain dependent natural language understanding. In *COLING-86*, 258–262.

1113. Muraki, Kazunori. 1982. On a semantic model for multi-lingual paraphrasing. In *COLING-82*, 239–244.

1114. Muraki, Kazunori, Shunji Ichiyama and Yasutomo Fukumochi. 1985. Augmented dependency grammar: a simple interface between the grammar rule and knowledge. In *ACL Proceedings, Second European Conference*, 198–204.

1115. Musha, Hiroyuki. 1986. A new predictive analyzer of English. In *COLING-86*, 470–472.

1116. Nadathur, Gopalan and Aravind K Joshi. 1983. Mutual beliefs in conversational systems: their role in referring expressions. In *IJCAI-83*, 603–605.

1117. Nadin, M. 1985. Review of T. Winograd, Language as a Cognitive Process. *Artificial Intelligence* 27:3, 353–356.

1118. Nagao, Makoto, Jun-ichi Tsujii, K. Mitamura, H. Hirakawa and M Kune. 1980. A machine translation system from Japanese into English: another perspective of MT systems. In *COLING-80*, 414–423.

1119. Nagao, Makoto, Jun-ichi Fujii, Y. Ueda and M Takiyama. 1980. An attempt to computerize dictionary data-bases. In *COLING-80*, 534–542.

1120. Nagao, Makoto, Jun-ichi Tsujii, K. Yada and T Kakimoto. 1982. An English Japanese machine translation system of the titles of scientific and engineering papers. In *COLING-82*, 245–252.

1121. Nagao, Makoto and Jun-ichi Nakamura. 1982. A parser which learns the application order of rewriting rules. In *COLING-82*, 253–258.

1122. Nagao, Makoto, Toyoaki Nishida and Jun-ichi Tsujii. 1984. Dealing with incompleteness of linguistic knowledge in language translation - transfer and generation stage of the Mu machine translation project. In *COLING-84*, 420–427.

1123. Nagao, Makoto and Jun-ichi Tsujii. 1986. The transfer phase of the Mu machine translation system. In *COLING-86*, 97–103.

1124. Nagao, Makoto. 1987. Role of structural transformation in a machine translation system. In *Machine Translation: Theoretical and Methodological Issues*, Sergei Nirenberg, (ed.) Cambridge University Press, Cambridge, 262–277.

1125. Naito, Shozo, Akira Shimazu and Hirosato Nomura. 1985. Classification of modality function and its application to Japanese. In *ACL Proceedings, 23rd Annual Meeting*, 27–34.

1126. Nakagawa, Sei-ichi. 1983. A recognition method of connected spoken words with syntactical constraints by augmented continuous DP algorithm. In *IJCAI-83*, 639–642.

1127. Nakamura, Jun-ichi, Jun-ichi Tsujii and Makoto Nagao. 1984. Grammar writing system (GRADE) of Mu-machine translation project and its characteristics. In *COLING-84*, 338–343.

1128. Nakamura, Jun-ichi, Jun-ichi Tsujii and Makoto Nagao. 1986. Solutions for problems of MT parser: methods used in Mu-machine translation project. In *COLING-86*, 133–135.

1129. Nakano, Hiroshi, Shin-ichi Tsuchiya and Akio Tsuruoka. 1980. An automatic processing of the natural language in the word count system. In *COLING-80*, 338–345.

1130. Nakhimovsky, Alexander. 1987. The lexicon, grammatical categories and temporal reasoning. In *Advances in Artificial Intelligence (Proceedings of AISB-87)*, Christopher S. Mellish and John Hallam, (eds.) Wiley, Chichester, 35–48.

1131. Narin'yani, Alexandre S. 1984. Towards an integral model of language competence. In *Computational Models of Natural Language Processing*, Bruno G. Bara and Giovanni Guida, (eds.) North-Holland, Amsterdam, 275–295.

1132. Narin'yani, Alexandre S. and O.P Simonova. 1985. The structure of communicative context of dialogue interaction. In *ACL Proceedings, Second European Conference*, 274–276.

1133. Nelimarkka, Esa, Harri Jäppinen and Aarno Lehtola. 1984. Two-way finite automata dependency grammar: a parsing method for inflectional free word order languages. In *COLING-84*, 389–392.

1134. Nelimarkka, Esa, Harri Jäppinen and Aarno Lehtola. 1984. Parsing an inflectional free word order language with two-way finite automata. In *ECAI-84*, 167–176.

1135. Nelimarkka, Esa, Harri Jäppinen and Aarno Lehtola. 1985. Parsing an inflectional free word order language with two-way finite automata. In *Advances in Artificial Intelligence*, Tim O'Shea, (ed.) North-Holland, Amsterdam, 325–334.

1136. Netter, Klaus. 1986. Getting things out of order (an LFG-proposal for the treatment of German word order). In *COLING-86*, 494–496.

1137. Neubert, G. 1982. Zum Wiederauffinden von Informationen in automatischen Wörterbüchern. In *COLING-82*, 259–264.

1138. Neuhaus, H. Joachim. 1986. Lexical database design: the Shakespeare dictionary model. In *COLING-86*, 441–444.

1139. Neumann, Bernd and Hans-Joachim Novak. 1983. Event models for recognition and natural language description of events in real-world image sequences. In *IJCAI-83*, 724–726.

1140. Niedermaier, Gerh.Th. 1986. Divided and valency-oriented parsing in speech understanding. In *COLING-86*, 593–595.

1141. Niimi, Yasuhisa, Shigeru Uzuhara and Yutaka Kobayashi. 1986. The procedure to construct a word predictor in a speech understanding system from a task-specific grammar defined in a CFG or a DCG. In *COLING-86*, 605–607.

1142. Nikolova, B. and I Nenova. 1982. Termservice - an automated system for terminology services. In *COLING-82*, 265–269.

1143. Nirenberg, Sergei. 1987. Knowledge and choices in machine translation. In *Machine Translation: Theoretical and Methodological Issues*, Sergei Nirenberg, (ed.) Cambridge University Press, Cambridge, 1–21.

1144. Nirenberg, Sergei, Victor Raskin and Allen B Tucker. 1987. The structure of interlingua in translator. In *Machine Translation: Theoretical and Methodological Issues*, Sergei Nirenberg, (ed.) Cambridge University Press, Cambridge, 90–113.

1145. Nirenberg, Sergei, (ed.) 1987. *Machine Translation: Theoretical and Methodological Issues*. Cambridge University Press, Cambridge.

1146. Nirenburg, Sergei. 1984. Interruptable transition networks. In *COLING-84*, 393–397.

1147. Nirenburg, Sergei and Victor Raskin. 1986. A metric for computational analysis of meaning: toward an applied theory of linguistic semantics. In *COLING-86*, 338–240.

1148. Nirenburg, Sergei, Victor Raskin and Allen B Tucker. 1986. On knowledge-based machine translation. In *COLING-86*, 627–632.

1149. Nishida, Fujio, Shinobu Takamatsu and Hiroaki Kuroki. 1980. English-Japanese translation through case-structure conversion. In *COLING-80*, 447–454.

1150. Nishida, Fujio and Shinobu Takamatsu. 1982. Japanese-English translation through internal expressions. In *COLING-82*, 271–276.

1151. Nishida, Fujio, Shinobu Takamatsu, Tadaaki Tani and Hiroji Kusaka. 1986. Text analysis and knowledge extraction. In *COLING-86*, 241–243.

1152. Nishida, Fujio, Yoneharu Fujita and Shinobu Takamatsu. 1986. Construction of a modular and portable translation system. In *COLING-86*, 649–651.

1153. Nishida, Toyoaki and Shuji Doshita. 1980. Hierarchical meaning representation and analysis of natural language documents. In *COLING-80*, 85–92.

1154. Nishida, Toyoaki, Masaki Kiyono and Shuji Doshita. 1981. An English-Japanese machine translation system based on formal semantics of natural language. In *Formal Approaches to Natural Language*, Shogo Iguchi, (ed.) Kyoto Working Group of Montague Grammar, Kyoto, 104–147.

1155. Nishida, Toyoaki and Shuji Doshita. 1982. An English-Japanese machine translation system based on formal semantics of natural language. In *COLING-82*, 277–282.

1156. Nishida, Toyoaki and Shuji Doshita. 1983. An application of Montague grammar to English-Japanese machine translation. In *ACL Proceedings, Conference on Applied Natural Language Processing*, 156–165.

1157. Nishida, Toyoaki and Shuji Doshita. 1984. Combining functionality and object-orientedness for natural language processing. In *COLING-84*, 218–221.

1158. Nitta, Yoshihiko, Atsushi Okajima, F. Yamano and K Ishihara. 1982. A heuristic approach to English-into-Japanese machine translation. In *COLING-82*, 283–288.

1159. Nitta, Yoshihiko, Atsushi Okajima, Hiroyuki Kaji and Youichi Hidano. 1984. A proper treatment of syntax and semantics in machine translation. In *COLING-84*, 159–166.

1160. Nitta, Yoshihiko. 1986. Idiosyncratic gap: a tough problem to structure-bound machine translation. In *COLING-86*, 107–111.

1161. Nohozoor-Farshi, R. 1987. Context-freeness of the language accepted by Marcus' Parser. In *ACL Proceedings, 25th Annual Meeting*, 117–122.

1162. Noll, A. Michael. 1980. Natural language interaction with machines. In *ACL Proceedings, 18th Annual Meeting*, 137–138.

1163. Nomura, Hirosato, Shozo Naito, Yasuhiro Katagiri and Akira Shimazu. 1986. Translation by understanding: a machine translation system LUTE. In *COLING-86*, 621–626.

1164. Norvig, Peter. 1983. Frame activated inferences in a story understanding program. In *IJCAI-83*, 624–626.

1165. Norvig, Peter. 1985. Review of G. Lakoff and Mark Johnson, Metaphors We Live By. *Artificial Intelligence* 27:3, 357–362.

1166. Norvig, Peter. 1987. Inference in text-understanding. In *AAAI-87*, 561–565.

1167. Novak, Hans-Joachim. 1986. Generating a coherent text describing a traffic scene. In *COLING-86*, 570–575.

1168. Nozohoor-Farshi, R. 1986. On formalizations of Marcus' parser. In *COLING-86*, 533–535.

1169. Nunberg, Geoffrey. 1987. Poetic and prosaic metaphors. In *TINLAP-3*, 177–180.

1170. Nunberg, Geoffrey. 1987. Position paper on common-sense and formal semantics. In *TINLAP-3*, 00–00.

1171. O'Kane, Mary. 1983. The FOPHO speech recognition project. In *IJCAI-83*, 630–632.

1172. O'Rorke, Paul. 1983. Reasons for beliefs in understanding: applications of non-monotonic dependencies to story processing. In *AAAI-83*, 306–309.

1173. Oakey, S. and R.C Cawthorn. 1981. Inductive learning of pronunciation rules by hypothesis testing and correction. *IJCAI-81* 1, 109–114.

1174. Ogawa, Hitoshi, Junichiro Ogawa and Kokichi Tanaka. 1980. The knowledge representation for a story understanding and simulation system. In *COLING-80*, 151–158.

1175. Ohyama, Yukata, Toshikazu Fukushima, Tomoki Shutoh and Masamichi Shutoh. 1986. A sentence analysis method for a Japanese book reading machine for the blind. In *ACL Proceedings, 24th Annual Meeting*, 165–172.

1176. Okada, Naoyuki. 1980. Conceptual taxonomy of Japanese verbs for understanding natural language and picture patterns. In *COLING-80*, 127–135.

1177. Ortony, Andrew and Lynn Fainsilber. 1987. The role of metaphors in descriptions of emotions. In *TINLAP-3*, 160–163.

1178. Osherson, Daniel N., Michael Stob and Scott Weinstein. 1983. Formal theories of language acquisition: practical and theoretical perspectives. In *IJCAI-83*, 566–572.

1179. Osherson, Daniel N. 1985. Computer output. *Cognition* 20, 261–264.

1180. Ott, Nikolaus and Magdalena Zoeppritz. 1980. USL- an experimental information system based on natural language. In *Natural Language Based Computer Systems*, Leonard Bolc, (ed.) Hanser, Munich, 255–284.

1181. Oubine, I.I. and B.D Tikhomirov. 1982. Machine translation systems and computer dictionaries in the information service: ways of their development and operation. In *COLING-82*, 289–294.

1182. Overmeier, Klaus K. 1985. Temporal inferences in medical texts. In *ACL Proceedings, 23rd Annual Meeting*, 9–17.

1183. Öhman, Sven. 1982. Discussion of Roger C. Schank's paper. In *Text Processing: Text Analysis and Generation, Text Typology and Attribution*, Sture Allén, (ed.) Almqvist and Wiksell, Stockholm, 75–83.

1184. Palmer, Martha S. 1981. A case for rule-driven semantic processing. In *ACL Proceedings, 19th Annual Meeting*, 125–131.

1185. Palmer, Martha S. 1983. Inference-driven semantic analysis. In *AAAI-83*, 310–313.

1186. Palmer, Martha S., Deborah A. Dahl, Rebecca J. Schiffman, Lynette Hirschman, Marcia Linebarger and John Dowding. 1986. Recovering implicit information. In *ACL Proceedings, 24th Annual Meeting*, 10–19.

1187. Panevová, Jarmila. 1984.   Natural language interface to an expert system. In *Artificial Intelligence and Information-Control Systems of Robots*, Ivan Plander, (ed.) North-Holland, Amsterdam, 277–280.

1188. Panevovà, J. 1982.   Random generation of Czech sentences. In *COLING-82*, 295–300.

1189. Papegaaij, Bart C., Victor Sadler and A.P.M Witkam. 1986. Experiments with an MT-directed lexical knowledge bank. In *COLING-86*, 432–434.

1190. Papegaaij, Bart C., Victor Sadler and Toon Witkam. 1986.   *Word Expert Semantics: An Interlingual Knowledge-Based Approach.* Foris, Dordrecht.

1191. Papp, F. 1982.   Empirical data and automatic analysis. In *COLING-82*, 301–306.

1192. Pareschi, Remo and Mark J Steedman. 1987.   A lazy way to chart-parse with categorial grammars. In *ACL Proceedings, 25th Annual Meeting*, 81–88.

1193. Paris, Cecile L. 1985.   Description strategies for naive and expert users. In *ACL Proceedings, 23rd Annual Meeting*, 238–245.

1194. Paris, Cecile L. 1987.   Combining discourse strategies to generate descriptions to users along a naive/expert spectrum. *IJCAI-87* 2, 626–632.

1195. Parisi, Domenico and Alessandra Giorgi. 1985.   GEMS: a model of sentence production. In *ACL Proceedings, Second European Conference*, 258–262.

1196. Parkinson, Roger C., Kenneth M. Colby and William S Faught. 1986 (1977).   Conversational language comprehension using integrated pattern-matching and parsing. In *Readings in Natural Language Processing*, Barbara J. Grosz, Karen Sparck-Jones and Bonnie Lynn Webber, (eds.) Morgan Kaufmann, Los Altos, 551–562.

1197. Passoneau, Rebecca J. 1987.   Situations and intervals. In *ACL Proceedings, 25th Annual Meeting*, 16–24.

1198. Patten, Terry. 1985.   A problem solving approach to generating text from systemic grammars. In *ACL Proceedings, Second European Conference*, 251–257.

1199. Pause, Peter E. 1984.   The interpretation of anaphoric expressions in Con-3-Tra. In *ECAI-84*, 232.

1200. Pazzani, Michael J. 1983.   Interactive script instantiation. In *AAAI-83*, 320–324.

1201. Pazzani, Michael J. and Carl Engelman. 1983.   Knowledge based question answering. In *ACL Proceedings, Conference on Applied Natural Language Processing*, 73–80.

1202. Pazzani, Michael J. 1984. Conceptual analysis of garden-path sentences. In *COLING-84*, 486–490.

1203. Pelletier, Bertrand and Jean Vaucher. 1986. GENIAL: un gènèrateur d'interface en langue naturelle. In *Proceedings of the 6th Canadian Conference on Artificial Intelligence*, 235–239.

1204. Pelletier, Francis J. 1980. Formal properties of rule orderings in linguistics. In *COLING-80*, 412–413.

1205. Pelletier, Francis J. and Lenhart K Schubert. 1984. Two theories for computing the logical form of mass expressions. In *COLING-84*, 108–111.

1206. Pereira, Fernando C.N. and David H.D Warren. 1986 (1980). Definite clause grammars for language analysis. In *Readings in Natural Language Processing*, Barbara J. Grosz, Karen Sparck-Jones and Bonnie Lynn Webber, (eds.) Morgan Kaufmann, Los Altos, 101–124.

1207. Pereira, Fernando C.N. 1980. Extraposition grammars. In *Proceedings of the First International Workshop on Logic Programming*, Sten-Ake Tarnlund, (ed.) Holms Gards Tryckeri, Debrecen, Hungary, 231–242.

1208. Pereira, Fernando C.N. and David H.D Warren. 1980. Definite clause grammars for language analysis - a survey of the formalism and a comparison with augmented transition networks. *Artificial Intelligence* 13:3, 231–278.

1209. Pereira, Fernando C.N. 1981. Extraposition grammars. *American Journal of Computational Linguistics* 7:4, 243–256.

1210. Pereira, Fernando C.N. and David H.D Warren. 1983. Parsing as deduction. In *ACL Proceedings, 21st Annual Meeting*, 137–144.

1211. Pereira, Fernando C.N. and Stuart M Shieber. 1984. The semantics of grammar formalisms seen as computer languages. In *COLING-84*, 123–129.

1212. Pereira, Fernando C.N. 1985. A new characterization of attachment preferences. In *Natural Language Parsing*, David R. Dowty, Lauri Karttunen and Arnold M. Zwicky, (eds.) Cambridge University Press, Cambridge, 307–319.

1213. Pereira, Fernando C.N. 1985. Parsing and deduction. In *Proceedings of an International Workshop on Natural Language Understanding and Logic Programming, University of Rennes.*

1214. Pereira, Fernando C.N. 1985. Deductive computation of grammar properties. In *Theoretical Approaches to Natural Language Understanding, a Workshop at Halifax, Nova Scotia*, 31.

1215. Pereira, Fernando C.N. 1985. A structure-sharing representation for unification-based grammar formalisms. In *ACL Proceedings, 23rd Annual Meeting*, 137–144.

1216. Pereira, Fernando C.N. 1987. Information, unification, and locality. In *TINLAP-3*, 32–36.

1217. Pereira, Fernando C.N. and Stuart M Shieber. 1987. *Prolog and Natural-Language Analysis*. CSLI Lecture Notes, vol. 10, Chicago University Press, Stanford.

1218. Pereira, Luis M., Paul Sabatier and Eugenio Oliveira. 1982. ORBI - an expert system for environmental resource evaluation through natural language. In *Proceedings of the First International Conference on Logic Programming*, Michel Van Caneghem, (ed.) Assocation pour la diffusion et le développement de PROLOG, Marseille, 200–209.

1219. Pericliev, Vladimir. 1984. Handling syntactical ambiguity in machine translation. In *COLING-84*, 521–524.

1220. Pericliev, Vladimir and Ilarion Ilarionov. 1986. Testing the projectivity hypothesis. In *COLING-86*, 56–58.

1221. Perrault, C. Raymond. 1986 (1984). On the mathematical properties of linguistic theories. In *Readings in Natural Language Processing*, Barbara J. Grosz, Karen Sparck-Jones and Bonnie Lynn Webber, (eds.) Morgan Kaufmann, Los Altos, 5–16.

1222. Perrault, C. Raymond and James F Allen. 1980. A plan-based analysis of indirect speech acts. *American Journal of Computational Linguistics* 6:3–4, 167–182.

1223. Perrault, C. Raymond and Philip R Cohen. 1981. It's for your own good: a note on inaccurate reference. In *Elements of Discourse Understanding*, Aravind K. Joshi, Bonnie Lynn Webber and Ivan Sag, (eds.) Cambridge University Press, Cambridge, 217–230.

1224. Perrault, C. Raymond. 1983. On the mathematical properties of linguistic theories. In *ACL Proceedings, 21st Annual Meeting*, 98–105.

1225. Perrault, C. Raymond. 1984. On the mathematical properties of linguistic theories. *Computational Linguistics* 10:3–4, 165–176.

1226. Perrault, C. Raymond. 1987. Towards a semantic theory of discourse. In *TINLAP-3*, 93–96.

1227. Pershina, E.L. 1986. Elementary contracts as a pragmatic basis of language interaction. In *COLING-86*, 229–231.

1228. Petrick, Stanley R. 1981. Field testing the transformational question answering (TQA) system. In *ACL Proceedings, 19th Annual Meeting*, 35–36.

1229. Petrick, Stanley R. 1982. Theoretical/technical issues in natural language access to databases. In *ACL Proceedings, 20th Annual Meeting*, 51–56.

1230. Phelps, R. 1986. Review of Philip N. Johnson-Laird, Mental Models. *Artificial Intelligence* 28:3, 343–344.

1231. Phillips, Brian and James A Hendler. 1980. The impatient tutor: an integrated language understanding system. In *COLING-80*, 480–486.

1232. Phillips, Brian and James A Hendler. 1982. A message-passing control structure for text understanding. In *COLING-82*, 307–312.

1233. Phillips, Brian. 1983. An object-oriented parser for text understanding. In *IJCAI-83*, 690–692.

1234. Phillips, Brian. 1984. An object-oriented parser. In *Computational Models of Natural Language Processing*, Bruno G. Bara and Giovanni Guida, (eds.) North-Holland, Amsterdam, 297–321.

1235. Phillips, Brian, Michael J. Freiling, James H. Alexander, Steven L. Messick, Steve Rehfuss and Sheldon Nicholl. 1985. An eclectic approach to building natural language interfaces. In *ACL Proceedings, 23rd Annual Meeting*, 254–261.

1236. Phillips, John D. and Henry S Thompson. 1985. GPSGP - a parser for generalized phrase structure grammars. *Linguistics* 23:2, 245–261.

1237. Pierrehumbert, Janet B. 1983. Automatic recognition of intonation patterns. In *ACL Proceedings, 21st Annual Meeting*, 85–90.

1238. Pigott, Ian M. 1986. Essential requirements for a large-scale operational machine-translation system. *Computers and Translation* 1:2, 67–72.

1239. Pilato, Samuel F. and Robert C Berwick. 1985. Reversible automata and induction of the English auxiliary system. In *ACL Proceedings, 23rd Annual Meeting*, 70–75.

1240. Pinkal, Manfred. 1986. Definite noun phrases and the semantics of discourse. In *COLING-86*, 368–373.

1241. Pique, Jean F. and Paul Sabatier. 1982. An informative, adaptable and efficient natural language consultable database system. In *ECAI-82*, 250–254.

1242. Pique, Jean F. 1982. On a semantic representation of natural language sentences. In *Proceedings of the First International Conference on Logic Programming*, Michel Van Caneghem, (ed.) Assocation pour la diffusion et le développement de PROLOG, Marseille, 215–223.

1243. Plante, Pierre. 1980. Text analysis learning strategies. In *COLING-80*, 354–358.

1244. Plantinga, Edwin. 1987. Mental models and metaphor. In *TINLAP-3*, 164–172.

1245. Plátek, M. 1982. Composition of translation schemes with D-trees. In *COLING-82*, 313–318.

1246. Poesio, Massimo and Claudio Rullent. 1987. Modified caseframe parsing for speech understanding systems. *IJCAI-87* 2, 622–625.

1247. Polanyi, Livia and Remko J.H Scha. 1984. A syntactic approach to discourse semantics. In *COLING-84*, 413–419.

1248. Pollack, Jordan B. and David L Waltz. 1984. Parallel interpretation of natural language. In *Proceedings of the International Conference on Fifth Generation Computer Systems*, ICOT, Tokyo, 686–694.

1249. Pollack, Martha E. 1986. A model of plan inference that distinguishes between the beliefs of actors and observers. In *ACL Proceedings, 24th Annual Meeting*, 207–214.

1250. Pollard, Carl J. and Lewis G Creary. 1985. A computational semantics for natural language. In *ACL Proceedings, 23rd Annual Meeting*, 172–179.

1251. Popov, E.V. 1986. *Talking with Computers in Natural Language*. Springer, Berlin.

1252. Popowich, Fred P. 1985. SAUMER: sentence analysis using metarules. In *ACL Proceedings, Second European Conference*, 48–56.

1253. Popowich, Fred P. 1985. Unrestricted gapping grammars. *IJCAI-85* 2, 765–768.

1254. Popowich, Fred P. 1985. Unrestricted gapping grammars for ID/LP grammars. In *Theoretical Approaches to Natural Language Understanding, a Workshop at Halifax, Nova Scotia*, 98–106.

1255. Popowich, Fred P. 1986. Unrestricted gapping grammars. *Computational Intelligence* 2:1, 28–53.

1256. Porter, Harry H. 1987. Incorporating inheritance and feature structures into a logic grammar formalism. In *ACL Proceedings, 25th Annual Meeting*, 228–234.

1257. Porto, Antonio and Miguel Figueiras. 1984. Natural language semantics: a logic programming approach. In *1984 International Symposium on Logic Programming*. IEEE Computer Society Press, Silver Spring, MD, 228–232.

1258. Porto, Antonio and M Filgueiras. 1984. Definite clause transition grammars. In *ISLP 84*, Atlantic City, N.J., 228–233.

1259. Postal, Paul M. and D. Terence Langendoen. 1984. English and the class of context-free languages. *Computational Linguistics* 10:3–4, 177–181.

1260. Pounder, Amande and Markus Kommenda. 1986. Morphological analysis for a German text-to-speech system. In *COLING-86*, 263–268.

1261. Prideaux, Gary D. 1980. The role of perceptual strategies in the processing of English relative clause structures. In *COLING-80*, 60–66.

1262. Prince, Ellen F. 1981. On the inferencing of indefinite 'this' NPs. In *Elements of Discourse Understanding*, Aravind K. Joshi, Bonnie Lynn Webber and Ivan Sag, (eds.) Cambridge University Press, Cambridge, 231–250.

1263. Prodanof, Irina and Giacomo Ferrari. 1983. Extended access to the left context in an ATN parser. In *ACL Proceedings, First European Conference*, 58–65.

1264. Prodanof, Irina and Giacomo Ferrari. 1986. Generalized memory manipulation actions for parsing natural language. In *COLING-86*, 473–475.

1265. Proudian, Derek and Carl J Pollard. 1985. Parsing head-driven phrase structure grammar. In *ACL Proceedings, 23rd Annual Meeting*, 167–171.

1266. Prószéky, Gábor. 1986. Processing clinical narratives in Hungarian. In *COLING-86*, 365–367.

1267. Pullum, Geoffrey K. 1983. Context-freeness and the computer processing of human languages. In *ACL Proceedings, 21st Annual Meeting*, 1–6.

1268. Pullum, Geoffrey K. 1984. Syntactic and semantic parsability. In *COLING-84*, 112–122.

1269. Pullum, Geoffrey K. 1984. On two recent attempts to show that English is not a CFL. *Computational Linguistics* 10:3–4, 182–186.

1270. Pulman, Stephen G. 1980. Parsing and syntactic theory. In *COLING-80*, 54–59.

1271. Pulman, Stephen G. 1983. Trace theory, parsing and constraints. In *Parsing Natural Language*, Margaret King, (ed.) Academic Press, London, 171–196.

1272. Pulman, Stephen G. 1983. Generalized phrase structure grammar, Earley's algorithm, and the minimisation of recursion. In *Automatic Natural Language Parsing*, Karen Sparck-Jones and Yorick A. Wilks, (eds.) Ellis Horwood/Wiley, Chichester/New York, 117–131.

1273. Pulman, Stephen G. 1984. Limited domain systems for language teaching. In *COLING-84*, 84–87.

1274. Pulman, Stephen G. 1985. A parser that doesn't. In *ACL Proceedings, Second European Conference*, 128–135.

1275. Pulman, Stephen G. 1985. The syntax-semantics interface. In *Proceedings of the Alvey/ICL Workshop on Linguistic Theory and Computer Applications*, Peter Whitelock, Harold Somers, Paul Bennett, Rod L. Johnson and Mary McGee Wood, (eds.) CCL/UMIST, Manchester, 120–145.

1276. Pulman, Stephen G. 1986. Grammars, parsers, and memory limitations. *Language and Cognitive Processes* 1, 197–225.

1277. Pulman, Stephen G. 1987. Events and VP modifiers. In *Proceedings of the Alvey Sponsored Workshop on Formal Semantics in Natural Language Processing*, Barry G.T. Lowden, (ed.) University of Essex, Colchester, 74–80.

1278. Pulman, Stephen G. 1987. Unification and the new grammatism. In *TINLAP-3*, 40–42.

1279. Pustejovsky, James. 1987. An integrated theory of discourse analysis. In *Machine Translation: Theoretical and Methodological Issues*, Sergei Nirenberg, (ed.) Cambridge University Press, Cambridge, 169–191.

1280. Pustejovsky, James and Sergei Nirenburg. 1987. On the acquisition of lexical entries: the perceptual orogins of thematic relations. In *ACL Proceedings, 25th Annual Meeting*, 172–178.

1281. Pustejovsky, James and Sergei Nirenburg. 1987. Lexical selection in the process of language generation. In *ACL Proceedings, 25th Annual Meeting*, 201–206.

1282. Pustejovsky, James and Sabine Berger. 1987. The acquisition of conceptual structure for the lexicon. In *AAAI-87*, 566–576.

1283. Quilici, Alexander E., Michael G. Dyer and Margot Flowers. AQUA: an intelligent UNIX advisor. *ECAI-86* 2, 33–38.

1284. Raccah, Pierre-Yves. 1984. Argumentation in representation semantics. In *COLING-84*, 525–529.

1285. Ralph, Bo. 1980. Relative semantic complexity in lexical units. In *COLING-80*, 115–121.

1286. Ram, Ashwin. 1987. AQUA Asking question and understanding answer. In *AAAI-87*, 313–316.

1287. Ramsay, Allan. 1980. Parsing English text. In *AISB-80*, 223–232.

1288. Ramsay, Allan. 1985. Effective parsing with generalized phrase structure grammar. In *ACL Proceedings, Second European Conference*, 57–61.

1289. Ramsay, Allan. 1986. Computer processing of natural language. In *Artificial Intelligence: Principles and Applications*, Masoud Yazdani, (ed.) Chapman and Hall, London, 69–110.

1290. Ramsay, Allan. 1987. Knowing that and knowing what. In *Advances in Artificial Intelligence (Proceedings of AISB-87)*, Christopher S. Mellish and John Hallam, (eds.) Wiley, Chichester, 279–290.

1291. Ramshaw, Lance A. and Ralph M Weischedel. 1984. Problem localization strategies for pragmatics processing in natural language front ends. In *COLING-84*, 139–143.

1292. Rankin, Ivan. 1986. SMORF - an implementation of Hellberg's morphology system. In *Papers from the Fifth Scandinavian Conference of Computational Linguistics*, Fred Karlsson, (ed.) University of Helsinki, Helsinki, 161–172.

1293. Rapaport, William J. and Stuart C Shapiro. 1984. Quasi-indexical reference in propositional semantic networks. In *COLING-84*, 65–70.

1294. Rapaport, William J. 1985. Meinongian semantics for propositional semantic networks. In *ACL Proceedings, 23rd Annual Meeting*, 43–48.

1295. Raskin, Victor. 1987. Linguistics and natural language processing. In *Machine Translation: Theoretical and Methodological Issues*, Sergei Nirenberg, (ed.) Cambridge University Press, Cambridge, 42–58.

1296. Rau, Lisa F. 1987. Information retrieval from never-ending stories. In *AAAI-87*.

1297. Rayner, Manny and Amelie Banks. 1986. Temporal relations and logic grammars. *ECAI-86* 2, 9–14.

1298. Razi, Amir M. 1985. Two strategies of robustness for natural language understanding systems. In *Humans and Machines: 4th Delaware Symposium on Language Studies*, Stephanie Williams, (ed.) Ablex, Norwood, 67–72.

1299. Reeker, Larry H., Elaine M. Zamora and Paul E Blower. 1983. Specialized information extraction: automatic chemical reaction coding from English descriptions. In *ACL Proceedings, Conference on Applied Natural Language Processing*, 109–116.

1300. Reichman, Rachel. 1981. Analogies in spontaneous discourse. In *ACL Proceedings, 19th Annual Meeting*, 63–69.

1301. Reichman, Rachel. 1981. Modeling informal debates. *IJCAI-81* 1, 19–24.

1302. Reichman, Rachel. 1985. *Getting Computers to Talk like You and Me: Discourse Context, Focus and Semantics (An ATN Model)*. MIT Press, Cambridge, Ma..

1303. Reichman-Adar, R. 1984. Extended person-machine interface. *Artificial Intelligence* 22:2, 157–218.

1304. Reilly, Ronan. 1984. A connectionist model of some aspects of anaphor resolution. In *COLING-84*, 144–149.

1305. Reiser, Brian J. 1981. Character tracking and the understanding of narratives. *IJCAI-81* 1, 209–211.

1306. Reiter, Raymond and Giovanni Criscuolo. 1983. Some representational issues in default reasoning. *Computers and Mathematics with Applications* 9:1, 15–27.

1307. Reply. 1982. Martin Kay. In *Text Processing: Text Analysis and Generation, Text Typology and Attribution*, Sture Allén, (ed.) Almqvist and Wiksell, Stockholm, 377–378.

1308. Reyle, Uwe and Werner Frey. 1983. A PROLOG implementation of lexical functional grammar. In *IJCAI-83*, 693–695.

1309. Reyle, Uwe. 1985. Grammatical functions, discourse, referents, and quantification. *IJCAI-85* 2, 829–831.

1310. Rich, Elaine, Jim Barnett, Kent Wittenburg and David A Wroblewski. 1987. Ambiguity procrastination. In *AAAI-87*, 571–576.

1311. Rieger, Burghard B. 1980. Fuzzy word meaning analysis and representation in linguistic semantics: an empirical approach to the reconstruction of lexical meanings in East- and West-German newspaper texts. In *COLING-80*, 76–84.

1312. Rieger, Burghard B. 1982. Procedural meaning representation by connotative dependency structures: an empirical approach to word semantics for analogical inferencing. In *COLING-82*, 319–324.

1313. Rieger, Burghard B. 1984. Semantic relevance and aspect dependency in a given subject domain. In *COLING-84*, 298–301.

1314. Riesbeck, Christopher K. 1981. Perspectives on parsing issues. In *ACL Proceedings, 19th Annual Meeting*, 105–106.

1315. Riesbeck, Christopher K. 1982. Realistic language comprehension. In *Strategies for Natural Language Processing*, Wendy G. Lehnert and Martin H. Ringle, (eds.) Erlbaum, Hillsdale, 37–54.

1316. Riesbeck, Christopher K. 1983. Some problems for conceptual analysers. In *Automatic Natural Language Parsing*, Karen Sparck-Jones and Yorick A. Wilks, (eds.) Ellis Horwood/Wiley, Chichester/New York, 178–181.

1317. Riesbeck, Christopher K. 1986. From conceptual analyzer to direct memory access parsing: An overview. In *Advances in Cognitive Science 1*, Noel E. Sharkey, (ed.) Ellis Horwood/Wiley, Chichester/New York, 236–258.

1318. Ringle, Martin H. and Bertram C Bruce. 1982. Conversation Failure. In *Strategies for Natural Language Processing*, Wendy G. Lehnert and Martin H. Ringle, (eds.) Erlbaum, Hillsdale, 203–221.

1319. Ristad, Eric Sven. 1986. Computational complexity of current GPSG theory. In *ACL Proceedings, 24th Annual Meeting*, 30–39.

1320. Ristad, Eric Sven. 1986. Defining natural language grammars in GPSG. In *ACL Proceedings, 24th Annual Meeting*, 40–44.

1321. Ristad, Eric Sven. 1987. Revised generalized phrase structure grammar. In *ACL Proceedings, 25th Annual Meeting*, 243–250.

1322. Ritchie, Graeme D. 1980. *Computational Grammar - an Artificial Intelligence Approach to linguistic description*. Harvester Press, Brighton.

1323. Ritchie, Graeme D. 1983. Semantics in parsing. In *Parsing Natural Language*, Margaret King, (ed.) Academic Press, London, 199–217.

1324. Ritchie, Graeme D. 1983. The implementation of a PIDGIN interpreter. In *Automatic Natural Language Parsing*, Karen Sparck-Jones and Yorick A. Wilks, (eds.) Ellis Horwood/Wiley, Chichester/New York, 69–80.

1325. Ritchie, Graeme D. 1984. A rational reconstruction of the PROTEUS sentence planner. In *COLING-84*, 327–329.

1326. Ritchie, Graeme D. 1984. Simulating a Turing machine using functional unification grammar. In *ECAI-84*, 127–136.

1327. Ritchie, Graeme D. and Henry S Thompson. 1984. Natural language processing. In *Artificial Intelligence: Tools, Techniques, and Applications*, Tim O'Shea and Marc Eisenstadt, (eds.) Harper & Row, New York, 358–388.

1328. Ritchie, Graeme D. 1985. The lexicon. In *Proceedings of the Alvey/ICL Workshop on Linguistic Theory and Computer Applications*, Peter Whitelock, Harold Somers, Paul Bennett, Rod L. Johnson and Mary McGee Wood, (eds.) CCL/UMIST, Manchester, 146–168.

1329. Ritchie, Graeme D. 1985. Simulating a Turing machine using functional unification grammar. In *Advances in Artificial Intelligence*, Tim O'Shea, (ed.) North-Holland, Amsterdam, 285–294.

1330. Ritchie, Graeme D. 1986. The computational complexity of sentence derivation in functional unification grammar. In *COLING-86*, 584–586.

1331. Robinson, Ann E. 1980. Interpreting verb phrase references in dialogs. In *Proceedings of the Third Biennial Conference of the Canadian Society for Computational Studies of Intelligence (3rd Canadian Conference on AI)*, 115–122.

1332. Robinson, Ann E. 1981. Determining verb phrase referents in dialogs. *American Journal of Computational Linguistics* 7:1, 1–16.

1333. Robinson, Jane J. 1986 (1982). DIAGRAM: a grammar for dialogues. In *Readings in Natural Language Processing*, Barbara J. Grosz, Karen Sparck-Jones and Bonnie Lynn Webber, (eds.) Morgan Kaufmann, Los Altos, 139–159.

1334. Robinson, Jane J. 1981. Perspectives on parsing issues. In *ACL Proceedings, 19th Annual Meeting*, 95–96.

1335. Rohrer, Christian. 1980. L'analyse logique des temps du passé en Francais. In *COLING-80*, 122–126.

1336. Rohrer, Christian. 1982. Towards a mechanical analysis of French tense forms in texts. In *COLING-82*, 331–332.

1337. Rohrer, Christian. 1986. Linguistic bases for machine translation. In *COLING-86*, 353–355.

1338. Root, Rebecca. 1985. A two-way approach to structural transfer in MT. In *ACL Proceedings, Second European Conference*, 70–72.

1339. Root, Rebecca. 1986. Semantics, translation, and anaphora. *Computers and Translation* 1:2, 93–108.

1340. Rosenberg, Jarrett. 1984. Lexical semantics in human-computer communication. In *COLING-84*, 428–431.

1341. Rosenberg, Richard S. 1980. Approaching discourse computationally: a review. In *Representation and Processing of Natural Language*, Leonard Bolc, (ed.) Hanser, Munich, 11–83.

1342. Rosenschein, Stanley J. 1981. Abstract theories of discourse and the formal specification of programs that converse. In *Elements of Discourse Understanding*, Aravind K. Joshi, Bonnie Lynn Webber and Ivan Sag, (eds.) Cambridge University Press, Cambridge, 251–265.

1343. Rosenschein, Stanley J. and Stuart M Shieber. 1982. Translating English into logical form. In *ACL Proceedings, 20th Annual Meeting*, 1–8.

1344. Rosner, Michael A. 1983. Production systems. In *Parsing Natural Language*, Margaret King, (ed.) Academic Press, London, 35–58.

1345. Ross, Kenneth M. 1982. An improved left-corner parsing algorithm. In *COLING-82*, 333–338.

1346. Rothkegel, Annely. 1986. Pragmatics in machine translation. In *COLING-86*, 335–337.

1347. Rounds, William C. and Alexis Manaster-Ramer. 1987. A logical version of functional grammar. In *ACL Proceedings, 25th Annual Meeting*, 89–96.

1348. Rösner, Dietmar F. and J.H Laubsch. 1982. Formalization of argumentation structures in newspaper texts. In *COLING-82*, 325–330.

1349. Rösner, Dietmar F. 1986. When Marion talks to Siegfried - experiences from a Japanese/German machine translation project. In *COLING-86*, 652–654.

1350. Rubinoff, Robert. 1986. Adapting MUMBLE: experience with natural language generation. *AAAI-86* 2, 1063–1068.

1351. Rumelhart, David E. and James L McClelland. 1986. On learning the past tense of English verbs. In *Parallel Distributed Processing*, James L. McClelland, David E. Rumelhart and the PDP Research Group, (eds.) vol. 2, MIT Press, Cambridge, Ma., 216–271.

1352. Russel, S. Weber. 1982. Formalising factors in metaphorical extension. In *ECAI-82*, 234–239.

1353. Russell, Graham J., Stephen G. Pulman, Graeme D. Ritchie and A.W Black. 1986. A dictionary and morphological analyser for English. In *COLING-86*, 277–279.

1354. Ruus, Hanne and Ebbe Spang-Hanssen. 1986. A theory of semantic relations for large scale natural language processing. In *COLING-86*, 20–22.

1355. Ryan, Karen L. 1981. Corepresentational grammar and parsing English comparatives. In *ACL Proceedings, 19th Annual Meeting*, 13–18.

1356. Sabah, Gérard and Mohamed Rady. 1983. A deterministic syntactic-semantic parser. In *IJCAI-83*, 707–709.

1357. Sabatier, Paul. 1985. Puzzle grammars. In *Natural Language Understanding and Logic Programming*, Veronica Dahl and Patrick Saint-Dizier, (eds.) North-Holland, Amsterdam, 139–152.

1358. Sabatier, Paul. 1985. Lexicon-grammars, a new deal for natural language compiling. In *Theoretical Approaches to Natural Language Understanding, a Workshop at Halifax, Nova Scotia*, 40–44.

1359. Sabot, Gary. 1986. Bulk processing of text on a massively parallel computer. In *ACL Proceedings, 24th Annual Meeting*, 128–135.

1360. Sag, Ivan A. 1983. Knowledge-based approaches. In *ACL Proceedings, Conference on Applied Natural Language Processing*, 54.

1361. Sager, Naomi. 1981. *Natural Language Information Processing: A Computer Grammar of English and its Applications*. Addison-Wesley, Reading, Ma..

1362. Sager, Naomi. 1986. *Medical Language Processing: Computer Management of Narrative Data*. Addison-Wesley, Reading, Ma..

1363. Saint-Dizier, Patrick. 1984. Quantifier hierarchy in a semantic representation of natural language sentences. In *ECAI-84*, 233.

1364. Saint-Dizier, Patrick. 1985. Handling quantifier scoping ambiguities in a semantic representation of natural language sentences. In *Natural Language Understanding and Logic Programming*, Veronica Dahl and Patrick Saint-Dizier, (eds.) North-Holland, Amsterdam, 49–63.

1365. Saint-Dizier, Patrick. 1985. A logic-based grammar for handling adjective phrases. In *Theoretical Approaches to Natural Language Understanding, a Workshop at Halifax, Nova Scotia*, 45–54.

1366. Saint-Dizier, Patrick. 1986. Expression of syntactic and semantic features in logic-based grammars. *Computational Intelligence* 2:1, 1–8.

1367. Sakamoto, Yoshiyuki and T Okamoto. 1982. Lexical parallelism in text structure determination and content analysis. In *COLING-82*, 339–344.

1368. Sakamoto, Yoshiyuki, Masayuki Satoh and Tetsuya Ishikawa. 1984. Lexicon features for Japanese syntactic analysis in Mu-project. In *COLING-84*, 42–47.

1369. Sakamoto, Yoshiyuki, Tetsuya Ishikawa and Masayuki Satoh. 1986. Concept and structure of semantic markers for machine translation in Mu-project. In *COLING-86*, 13–19.

1370. Salkoff, Morris. 1980. A context-free grammar of French. In *COLING-80*, 38–45.

1371. Salton, Gerard. 1985. On the representation of query term relations by soft Boolean operators. In *ACL Proceedings, Second European Conference*, 116–122.

1372. Salton, Gerard. 1986. On the use of term associations in automatic information retrieval. In *COLING-86*, 380–386.

1373. Salveter, Sharon C. 1980. On the existence of primitive meaning units. In *ACL Proceedings, 18th Annual Meeting*, 13–15.

1374. Salveter, Sharon C. and David Maier. 1982. Natural language updates. In *COLING-82*, 345–350.

1375. Salveter, Sharon C. and David Maier. 1982. Natural language database updates. In *ACL Proceedings, 20th Annual Meeting*, 67–73.

1376. Salveter, Sharon C. 1982. Inferring building blocks for knowledge representation. In *Strategies for Natural Language Processing*, Wendy G. Lehnert and Martin H. Ringle, (eds.) Erlbaum, Hillsdale, 327–344.

1377. Salveter, Sharon C. 1984. A model of action that supports natural language database update. In *ECAI-84*, 185–194.

1378. Salveter, Sharon C. 1985. A model of action that supports natural language database update. In *Advances in Artificial Intelligence*, Tim O'Shea, (ed.) North-Holland, Amsterdam, 257–266.

1379. Samad, Tariq. 1986. *A Natural Language for Computer-Aided Design*. Kluwer, Boston.

1380. Samet, Jerry and Roger C Schank. 1984. Coherence and connectivity. *Linguistics and Philosophy* 7, 57–82.

1381. Sampson, Geoffrey. 1983. Fallible rationalism and machine translation. In *ACL Proceedings, First European Conference*, 86–89.

1382. Sampson, Geoffrey. 1983. Deterministic parsing. In *Parsing Natural Language*, Margaret King, (ed.) Academic Press, London, 91–116.

1383. Sampson, Geoffrey. 1983. Context-free parsing and the adequacy of context-free grammars. In *Parsing Natural Language*, Margaret King, (ed.) Academic Press, London, 151–170.

1384. Sampson, Geoffrey. 1986. A stochastic approach to parsing. In *COLING-86*, 151–155.

1385. Sandewall, Erik. 1982. A note based on Martin Kay's paper. In *Text Processing: Text Analysis and Generation, Text Typology and Attribution*, Sture Allén, (ed.) Almqvist and Wiksell, Stockholm, 371–375.

1386. Sato, Taisuka. 1980. SGS: a system for mechanical generation of Japanese sentences. In *COLING-80*, 21–28.

1387. Sawai, S., H. Fukushima, M. Sugimoto and N Ukai. 1982. Knowledge representation and machine translation. In *COLING-82*, 351–356.

1388. Scha, Remko J.H. 1982. English words and data bases: how to bridge the gap. In *ACL Proceedings, 20th Annual Meeting*, 57–59.

1389. Schank, Roger C. 1986 (1980). Language and memory. In *Readings in Natural Language Processing*, Barbara J. Grosz, Karen Sparck-Jones and Bonnie Lynn Webber, (eds.) Morgan Kaufmann, Los Altos, 171–191.

1390. Schank, Roger C., Michael Lebowitz and Lawrence Birnbaum. 1980. An integrated understander. *American Journal of Computational Linguistics* 6:1, 13–30.

1391. Schank, Roger C. and Christopher K. Riesbeck, (eds.) 1981. *Inside Computer Understanding: Five Programs plus Miniatures*. Erlbaum, Hillsdale.

1392. Schank, Roger C. 1982. Representing meaning: an artificial intelligence perspective. In *Text Processing: Text Analysis and Generation, Text Typology and Attribution*, Sture Allén, (ed.) Almqvist and Wiksell, Stockholm, 25–63.

1393. Schank, Roger C. 1982. Reminding and organization: an introduction to MOPS. In *Strategies for Natural Language Processing*, Wendy G. Lehnert and Martin H. Ringle, (eds.) Erlbaum, Hillsdale, 455–493.

1394. Schank, Roger C. and Peter Childers. 1984. *The Cognitive Computer: On Language, Learning and Artificial Intelligence*. Addison-Wesley, Reading.

1395. Schank, Roger C. and Alex Kass. 1987. Natural language processing: what's really involved ?. In *TINLAP-3*, 101–105.

1396. Schenk, André. 1986. Idioms in the Rosetta machine translation system. In *COLING-86*, 319–324.

1397. Schlegloff, Emmanuel. 1980. What type of interaction is it to be. In *ACL Proceedings, 18th Annual Meeting*, 81–82.

1398. Schmidt, Paul. 1986. Valence theory in a stratificational MT-system. In *COLING-86*, 307–312.

1399. Schmucker, K.J. 1984. *Fuzzy Sets, Natural Language Computations, and Risk Analysis*. Computer Science Press, Rockville.

1400. Schnelle, Helmut. 1984. Concurrent parsing in programmable logic array (PLA) nets - proposals and problems. In *COLING-84*, 150–153.

1401. Schubert, Lenhart K. and Francis J Pelletier. 1986 (1982). From English to logic: context-free computation of 'conventional' logical translation. In *Readings in Natural Language Processing*, Barbara J. Grosz, Karen Sparck-Jones and Bonnie Lynn Webber, (eds.) Morgan Kaufmann, Los Altos, 293–311.

1402. Schubert, Lenhart K. and Francis J Pelletier. 1982. From English to logic: context-free computation of 'conventional' logical translation. *American Journal of Computational Linguistics* 8:1, 27–44.

1403. Schubert, Lenhart K. 1984. On parsing preferences. In *COLING-84*, 247–250.

1404. Schubert, Lenhart K. and L Watanabe. 1986. What's in an answer: a theoretical perspective on deductive question answering. In *Proceedings of the 6th Canadian Conference on Artificial Intelligence*, 71–77.

1405. Schubert, Lenhart K. 1986. Are there preference trade-offs in attachment decisions ?. *AAAI-86* 1, 601–605.

1406. Schuster, Ethel and Timothy W Finis. 1985. VP2: the role of user modelling in correcting errors in second language learning. In *AISB-85*, 187–195.

1407. Schuster, Ethel. 1986. The role of native grammars in correcting errors in second language learning. *Computational Intelligence* 2:2, 93–98.

1408. Schwind, Camilla B. 1985. Logic based natural language processing. In *Natural Language Understanding and Logic Programming*, Veronica Dahl and Patrick Saint-Dizier, (eds.) North-Holland, Amsterdam, 207–219.

1409. Sebastiani, Fabrizio, Giacomo Ferrari and Irina Prodanof. 1986. Semantic interpretation of technical texts. *ECAI-86* 2, 15–22.

1410. Sedelow, Sally Yeates and Walter A. Sedelow, Jr. 1986. The lexicon in the background. *Computers and Translation* 1:2, 73–82.

1411. Sedogbo, Célestin. 1985. A meta-grammar for handling coordination in logic grammars. In *Natural Language Understanding and Logic Programming*, Veronica Dahl and Patrick Saint-Dizier, (eds.) North-Holland, Amsterdam, 153–163.

1412. Sedogbo, Célestin. 1986. Extending the expressive capacity of the semantic component of the OPERA system. In *COLING-86*, 23–28.

1413. Sedogdo, Célestin. 1985. A meta-grammar for handling coordination in logic grammars. In *Proceedings of an International Workshop on Natural Language Understanding and Logic Programming, University of Rennes*.

1414. Segre, Alberto Maria, Bruce Arne Sherwood and Wayne B Dickerson. 1983. An expert system for the production of phoneme strings from unmarked English text using machine-induced rules. In *ACL Proceedings, First European Conference*, 35–42.

1415. Seidenberg, Mark S. and Michael K Tanenhaus. 1980. Chronometric studies of lexical ambiguity resolution. In *ACL Proceedings, 18th Annual Meeting*, 155–157.

1416. Sejnowski, Terrence J. 1986. Language learning in massively-parallel networks. In *ACL Proceedings, 24th Annual Meeting*, 184.

1417. Selfridge, Mallory. 1980. A computer model of child language learning. In *AAAI-80*, 224–227.

1418. Selfridge, Mallory. 1981. A computer model of child language acquisition. *IJCAI-81* 1, 92–96.

1419. Selfridge, Mallory. 1982. Inference and learning in a computer model of the development of language comprehension in a young child. In *Strategies for Natural Language Processing*, Wendy G. Lehnert and Martin H. Ringle, (eds.) Erlbaum, Hillsdale, 299–326.

1420. Selfridge, Mallory. 1982. Why do children misunderstand reversible passives? the CHILD program learns to understand passive sentences. In *AAAI-82*, 251–254.

1421. Selfridge, Mallory. 1986. A computer model of child language learning. *Artificial Intelligence* 29:2, 171–216.

1422. Selfridge, Mallory. 1986. Integrated processing produces robust understanding. *Computational Linguistics* 12:2, 89–106.

1423. Sembugamoorthy, V. 1981. Analogy-based acquisition of utterances relating to temporal aspects. *IJCAI-81* 1, 106–108.

1424. Seppänen, Jouko J. 1980. Soft display key for Kanji input. In *COLING-80*, 287–294.

1425. Sgall, Petr. 1982. Natural language understanding and the perspectives of question answering. In *COLING-82*, 357–364.

1426. Sgall, Petr. 1982. Automatic understanding with a linguistically based knowledge representation. In *ECAI-82*, 240–243.

1427. Sgall, Petr. 1984. Artificial Intelligence and semantics. In *Artificial Intelligence and Information-Control Systems of Robots*, Ivan Plander, (ed.) North-Holland, Amsterdam, 329–332.

1428. Shalyapina, Z.M. 1980. Problems of formal representation of text structure from the point of view of automatic translation. In *COLING-80*, 174–182.

1429. Shann, Patrick and J.L Cochard. 1984. GTT: a general transducer for teaching computational linguistics. In *COLING-84*, 88–91.

1430. Shapiro, Stuart C. and Jeannette G Neal. 1982. A knowledge engineering approach to natural language understanding. In *ACL Proceedings, 20th Annual Meeting*, 136–144.

1431. Shapiro, Stuart C. 1982. Generalized augmented transition network grammars for generation from semantic networks. *American Journal of Computational Linguistics* 8:1, 12–26.

1432. Sharp, Randall. 1986. A parametric NL translator. In *COLING-86*, 124–126.

1433. Shastri, Lokendra and Jerome A Feldman. 1986. Neural nets, routines, and semantic networks. In *Advances in Cognitive Science 1*, Noel E. Sharkey, (ed.) Ellis Horwood/Wiley, Chichester/New York, 158–203.

1434. Shieber, Stuart M. 1983. Sentence disambiguation by a shift-reduce parsing technique. In *IJCAI-83*, 699–703.

1435. Shieber, Stuart M., Susan U. Stucky, Hans Uszkoreit and Jane J Robinson. 1983. Formal constraints on metarules. In *ACL Proceedings, 21st Annual Meeting*, 22–27.

1436. Shieber, Stuart M. 1983. Sentence disambiguation by a shift-reduce parsing technique. In *ACL Proceedings, 21st Annual Meeting*, 113–118.

1437. Shieber, Stuart M. 1984. The design of a computer language for linguistic information. In *COLING-84*, 362–366.

1438. Shieber, Stuart M. 1984. Direct parsing of ID/LP grammars. *Linguistics and Philosophy* 7, 135–154.

1439. Shieber, Stuart M. 1985. Criteria for designing computer facilities for linguistic analysis. *Linguistics* 23:2, 189–211.

1440. Shieber, Stuart M. 1985. Separating linguistic analyses from linguistic theories. In *Proceedings of the Alvey/ICL Workshop on Linguistic Theory and Computer Applications*, Peter Whitelock, Harold Somers, Paul Bennett, Rod L. Johnson and Mary McGee Wood, (eds.) CCL/UMIST, Manchester, 2–26.

1441. Shieber, Stuart M. 1985. Using restriction to extend parsing algorithms for complex-feature-based formalisms. In *ACL Proceedings, 23rd Annual Meeting*, 145–152.

1442. Shieber, Stuart M. 1986. A simple reconstruction of GPSG. In *COLING-86*, 211–215.

1443. Shieber, Stuart M. 1986. *An Introduction to Unification-Based Approaches to Grammar*. University of Chicago Press, Chicago.

1444. Shigenaga, Minoru, Yoshihiro Sekiguchi and Chia-horng Lai. 1980. Speech recognition system for spoken Japanese sentences. In *COLING-80*, 472–479.

1445. Shimazu, Akira, Shozo Naito and Hirosato Nomura. 1983. Japanese language semantic analyzer based on an extended case frame model. In *IJCAI-83*, 717–720.

1446. Shimazu, Akira, Shozo Naito and Hirosato Nomura. 1987. Semantic structure analysis of Japanese noun phrases. In *ACL Proceedings, 25th Annual Meeting*, 123–130.

1447. Shimomura, Takeshi. 1980. Science of the stroke sequence of Kanji. In *COLING-80*, 270–273.

1448. Shirai, Hidetoshi. 1980. How to deal with ambiguities while parsing: EXAM - a semantic processing system for Japanese language. In *COLING-80*, 368–373.

1449. Shirai, K., Y. Fukazawa, T. Matzui and H Matzuura. 1980. A trial of Japanese text input system using speech recognition. In *COLING-80*, 464–471.

1450. Shirai, K. and T Hamada. 1986. Linguistic knowledge extraction from real language behavior. In *COLING-86*, 253–255.

1451. Shneiderman, Ben. 1980. Natural vs. precise language for human operation of computers. In *ACL Proceedings, 18th Annual Meeting*, 139–141.

1452. Shudo, Kosho, Toshiko Narahara and Sho Yoshida. 1980. Morphological aspect of Japanese language processing. In *COLING-80*, 1–8.

1453. Shwartz, Steven P. 1982. Problems with domain-independent natural language database access systems. In *ACL Proceedings, 20th Annual Meeting*, 60–62.

1454. Sidner, Candace L. 1986 (1983). Focusing in the comprehension of definite anaphora. In *Readings in Natural Language Processing*, Barbara J. Grosz, Karen Sparck-Jones and Bonnie Lynn Webber, (eds.) Morgan Kaufmann, Los Altos, 363–394.

1455. Sidner, Candace L. and David J Israel. 1981. Recognizing intended meaning and speakers' plans. *IJCAI-81* 1, 203–208.

1456. Sidner, Candace L. 1981. Focusing for interpretation of pronouns. *American Journal of Computational Linguistics* 7:4, 217–231.

1457. Sidner, Candace L. 1983. What the speaker means: recognition of speakers' plans in discourse. *Computers and Mathematics with Applications* 9:1, 71–82.

1458. Sidner, Candace L. 1983. Focusing in the comprehension of definite anaphora. In *Computational Models of Discourse*, Michael Brady and Robert C. Berwick, (eds.) MIT Press, Cambridge, Ma., 267–330.

1459. Sidner, Candace L. 1985. Plan parsing for intended response recognition in discourse. In *Theoretical Approaches to Natural Language Understanding, a Workshop at Halifax, Nova Scotia*, 39.

1460. Sidner, Candace L. 1985. Plan parsing for intended response recognition in discourse. *Computational Intelligence* 1:1, 1–10.

1461. Sigurd, Bengt. 1982. Commentator: a computer model of verbal production. *Linguistics* 20:9/10, 611–632.

1462. Sigurd, Bengt. 1982. Text representation in a text production model. In *Text Processing: Text Analysis and Generation, Text Typology and Attribution*, Sture Allén, (ed.) Almqvist and Wiksell, Stockholm, 135–152.

1463. Sigurd, Bengt. 1984. Computer simulation of spontaneous speech production. In *COLING-84*, 79–83.

1464. Sigurd, Bengt. 1986. Computer simulation of dialogue and communication. In *Papers from the Fifth Scandinavian Conference of Computational Linguistics*, Fred Karlsson, (ed.) University of Helsinki, Helsinki, 173–184.

1465. Simmons, Robert F. 1980. Word, phrase, and sentence. In *ACL Proceedings, 18th Annual Meeting*, 145–146.

1466. Simmons, Robert F. 1982. A narrative schema in procedural logic. In *Logic Programming*, Keith L. Clark and Sten-Ake Tarnlund, (eds.) Academic Press, London, 67–80.

1467. Simmons, Robert F. 1982. Themes from 1972. In *ACL Proceedings, 20th Annual Meeting*, 100–101.

1468. Simmons, Robert F. 1983. *Computations from the English*. Prentice Hall, Englewood Cliffs.

1469. Simmons, Robert F. 1984. The costs of inheritance in semantic networks. In *COLING-84*, 71–74.

1470. Sjoberg, Margareta. 1986. On the identification of stems in FASS. In *Papers from the Fifth Scandinavian Conference of Computational Linguistics*, Fred Karlsson, (ed.) University of Helsinki, Helsinki, 185–194.

1471. Slack, Jon M. 1980. Metaphor comprehension - a special mode of language processing ?. In *ACL Proceedings, 18th Annual Meeting*, 23–24.

1472. Slack, Jon M. 1984. A parsing architecture based on distributed memory machines. In *COLING-84*, 92–95.

1473. Slack, Jon M. 1984. The role of distributed memory in natural language parsing. In *ECAI-84*, 379–388.

1474. Slack, Jon M. 1985. The role of distributed memory in natural language parsing. In *Advances in Artificial Intelligence*, Tim O'Shea, (ed.) North-Holland, Amsterdam, 169–178.

1475. Slack, Jon M. 1986. Distributed memory: a basis for chart parsing. In *COLING-86*, 476–481.

1476. Slocum, Jonathan. 1980. An experiment in machine translation. In *ACL Proceedings, 18th Annual Meeting*, 163–167.

1477. Slocum, Jonathan. 1981. A practical comparison of parsing strategies. In *ACL Proceedings, 19th Annual Meeting*, 1–6.

1478. Slocum, Jonathan. 1983. A status report on the LRC machine translation system. In *ACL Proceedings, Conference on Applied Natural Language Processing*, 166–173.

1479. Slocum, Jonathan. 1984. Machine translation: its history, current status and future prospects. In *COLING-84*, 546–561.

1480. Slocum, Jonathan, Winfield S. Bennett, Lesley Whiffin and Edda Norcross. 1985. An evaluation of METAL: the LRC machine translation system. In *ACL Proceedings, Second European Conference*, 62–69.

1481. Slocum, Jonathan. 1985. A survey of machine translation: its history, current status, and future prospects. *Computational Linguistics* 11:1, 1–17.

1482. Small, Steven L. 1981. Viewing word expert parsing as linguistic theory. *IJCAI-81* 1, 70–76.

1483. Small, Steven L. and Chuck Rieger. 1982. Parsing and comprehending with word experts (a theory and its realization). In *Strategies for Natural Language Processing*, Wendy G. Lehnert and Martin H. Ringle, (eds.) Erlbaum, Hillsdale, 89–147.

1484. Small, Steven L., Garrison W. Cottrell and Lokendra Shastri. 1982. Toward connectionist parsing. In *AAAI-82*, 247–250.

1485. Small, Steven L. 1983. Parsing as co-operative distributional inference. Understanding through memory interactions. In *Parsing Natural Language*, Margaret King, (ed.) Academic Press, London, 247–276.

1486. Smith, Brian C. 1982. Linguistic and computational semantics. In *ACL Proceedings, 20th Annual Meeting*, 9–15.

1487. Smith, M. Cassandra Foster. 1980. Efficiency tools in the speeches of Martin Luther King Jr.. In *COLING-80*, 167–173.

1488. Somers, Harold L. 1982. The use of verb features in arriving at a meaning representation. *Linguistics* 20:3/4, 237–265.

1489. Somers, Harold L. 1983. Investigating the possibility of a microprocessor-based machine translation system. In *ACL Proceedings, Conference on Applied Natural Language Processing*, 149–155.

1490. Somers, Harold L. 1986. The need for MT-oriented versions of case and valency in MT. In *COLING-86*, 118–123.

1491. Somers, Harold L. 1986. *Valency and Case in Computational Linguistics*. Edinburgh University Press, Edinburgh.

1492. Sondheimer, Norman K. and Ralph M Weischedel. 1980. A rule-based approach to ill-formed input. In *COLING-80*, 46–53.

1493. Sondheimer, Norman K. 1981. Evaluation of natural language interfaces to database systems. In *ACL Proceedings, 19th Annual Meeting*, 29–30.

1494. Sondheimer, Norman K. 1982. On the present. In *ACL Proceedings, 20th Annual Meeting*, 107.

1495. Sondheimer, Norman K., Ralph M. Weischedel and Robert J Bobrow. 1984. Semantic interpretation using KL-ONE. In *COLING-84*, 101–107.

1496. Sondheimer, Norman K. and Bernhard Nebel. 1986. A logical-form and knowledge-base design for natural language generation. *AAAI-86* 1, 612–618.

1497. Sondheimer, Norman K. 1987. The rate of progress in natural language processing. In *TINLAP-3*, 106–109.

1498. Sosnowski, Zenon A. 1984. A method of the execution of fuzzy programs. In *Artificial Intelligence and Information-Control Systems of Robots*, Ivan Plander, (ed.) North-Holland, Amsterdam, 349–352.

1499. Soulhi, Said. 1984. Representing knowledge about knowledge and mutual knowledge. In *COLING-84*, 194–199.

1500. Sowa, John F. 1983. Generating language from conceptual graphs. *Computers and Mathematics with Applications* 9:1, 29–43.

1501. Sowa, John F. 1984. *Conceptual Structures: Information Processing in Mind and Machine*. Addison-Wesley, Reading.

1502. Sparck-Jones, Karen and Yorick A. Wilks, (eds.). *Automatic Natural Language Parsing*. Ellis Horwood/Wiley, Chichester/New York.

1503. Sparck-Jones, Karen. 1983. Shifting meaning representations. In *IJCAI-83*, 621-623.

1504. Sparck-Jones, Karen. 1983. So what about parsing compound nouns?. In *Automatic Natural Language Parsing*, Karen Sparck-Jones and Yorick A. Wilks, (eds.) Ellis Horwood/Wiley, Chichester/New York, 164-168.

1505. Sparck-Jones, Karen. 1984. Natural language and databases, again. In *COLING-84*, 182-183.

1506. Sparck-Jones, Karen and John I Tait. 1984. Linguistically motivated descriptive term selection. In *COLING-84*, 287-290.

1507. Sparck-Jones, Karen. 1985. Linguistic theory and beyond. In *Proceedings of the Alvey/ICL Workshop on Linguistic Theory and Computer Applications*, Peter Whitelock, Harold Somers, Paul Bennett, Rod L. Johnson and Mary McGee Wood, (eds.) CCL/UMIST, Manchester, 190-207.

1508. Sparck-Jones, Karen. 1986. *Synonymy and Semantic Classification*. Edinburgh University Press, Edinburgh.

1509. Sparck-Jones, Karen. 1987. Natural language processing. In *Intelligent Knowledge-Based Systems: An Introduction*, Tim O'Shea, John Self and Glan Thomas, (eds.) Harper & Row, London, 00-00.

1510. Sparck-Jones, Karen. 1987. They say it's a new sort of engine: but the SUMP's here to stay. In *TINLAP-3*, 119-122.

1511. Sparck-Jones, Karen and Branimir K Boguraev. 1987. A note on a study of cases. *Computational Linguistics* 13:1-2, 65-68.

1512. Sproat, Richard W. and Barbara Brunson. 1987. Constituent-based morphological parsing: a new approach to the problem of word-recognition. In *ACL Proceedings, 25th Annual Meeting*, 65-72.

1513. Sproat, Richard W. and Mark Liberman. 1987. Treating English nominals correctly. In *ACL Proceedings, 25th Annual Meeting*, 140-146.

1514. Srihari, Sargur N. and Jonathan J Hull. 1982. Knowledge integration in text recognition. In *AAAI-82*, 148-151.

1515. Stabler, Edward P., Jr. 1983. Deterministic and bottom-up parsing in PROLOG. In *AAAI-83*, 383-386.

1516. Stabler, Edward P., Jr. 1986. Restricting logic grammars. *AAAI-86* 2, 1048-1052.

1517. Stabler, Edward P., Jr. 1987. Restricting logic grammars with government-binding theory. *Computational Linguistics* 13:1–2, 1–10.

1518. Stallard, David. 1987. The logical analysis of lexical ambiguity. In *ACL Proceedings, 25th Annual Meeting*, 179–185.

1519. Stallard, David G. 1986. A terminological simplification transformation for natural language question-answering systems. In *ACL Proceedings, 24th Annual Meeting*, 241–246.

1520. Stanfill, Craig W. 1987. Memory-based reasoning applied to English pronounciation. In *AAAI-87*, 577–581.

1521. Stanta, A. Archi, B. Inghirami Jannucci, L. Parenti, G. Taddei Elmi, C. Biagioli, P. Mariani Biagini, F. Socci Natali and D Tiscornia. 1982. A linguistic tool for legal data retrieval. In *Deontic Logic, Computational Linguistics and Legal Information Systems*, Antonio A. Martino, (ed.) North-Holland, Amsterdam, 327–337.

1522. Starosta, Stanley and Hirosato Nomura. 1986. Lexicase parsing: a lexicon driven approach to syntactic analysis. In *COLING-86*, 127–132.

1523. Steedman, Mark J. and Philip N Johnson-Laird. 1980. The production of sentences, utterances and speech acts: have computers anything to say?. In *Language Production: Speech and Talk*, Brian Butterworth, (ed.) vol. 1, Academic Press, London, 111–141.

1524. Steedman, Mark J. and A Ades. 1980. An algorithmic account of English main clause constructions. In *AISB-80*, 259–268.

1525. Steedman, Mark J. 1983. Natural and unnatural language processing. In *Automatic Natural Language Parsing*, Karen Sparck-Jones and Yorick A. Wilks, (eds.) Ellis Horwood/Wiley, Chichester/New York, 132–140.

1526. Steel, Sam. 1984. Simplifying recursive belief for language understanding. In *ECAI-84*, 177–180.

1527. Steel, Sam and Anne N De Roeck. 1987. Bidirectional chart parsing. In *Advances in Artificial Intelligence (Proceedings of AISB-87)*, Christopher S. Mellish and John Hallam, (eds.) Wiley, Chichester, 223–235.

1528. Steinacker, Ingeborg and Harald Trost. 1982. Parsing German. In *COLING-82*, 365–370.

1529. Steinacker, Ingeborg and Ernst Buchberger. 1983. Relating syntax and semantics: the syntactic-semantic lexicon of the system VieLang. In *ACL Proceedings, First European Conference*, 96–100.

1530. Steinacker, Ingeborg and Harald Trost. 1983. Structural relations - a case against case. In *IJCAI-83*, 627–629.

1531. Steiner, Erich. 1986. Generating semantic structures in EURO-TRA-D. In *COLING-86*, 304–306.

1532. Stirling, Lesley. 1985. Distributives, quantifiers and a multiplicity of events. In *ACL Proceedings, Second European Conference*, 16–24.

1533. Stock, Oliviero, Cristiano Castelfranchi and Domenico Parisi. 1983. WEDNESDAY: parsing flexible word order languages. In *ACL Proceedings, First European Conference*, 106–110.

1534. Stock, Oliviero. 1986. Dynamic unification in lexically based parsing. *ECAI-86* 1, 212–221.

1535. Stock, Oliviero. 1987. Getting ideas into a lexicon based parser's head. In *ACL Proceedings, 25th Annual Meeting*, 52–58.

1536. Strzalkowski, Tomek and Nick Cercone. 1985. A framework for computing extra-sentential references. In *Theoretical Approaches to Natural Language Understanding, a Workshop at Halifax, Nova Scotia*, 107–116.

1537. Strzalkowski, Tomek. 1986. An approach to non-singular terms in discourse. In *COLING-86*, 362–364.

1538. Strzalkowski, Tomek. 1986. Representing conceptual dependency in discourse. In *Proceedings of the 6th Canadian Conference on Artificial Intelligence*, 57–61.

1539. Stucky, Susan U. 1987. A situated perspective on natural-language processing. In *TINLAP-3*, 123–127.

1540. Suen, C.Y. 1982. Computational analysis of Mandarin sounds with reference to the English language. In *COLING-82*, 371–376.

1541. Sugimura, R. 1986. Japanese honorifics and situation semantics. In *COLING-86*, 507–510.

1542. Sugita, Shigeharu. 1980. Text Processing of Thai language: the three seals law. In *COLING-80*, 330–337.

1543. Sugiyama, Kenji, Masayuki Kameda, Kouji Akiyama and Akifumi Makinouchi. 1984. Understanding of Japanese in an interactive programming system. In *COLING-84*, 385–388.

1544. Suzuki, H., Masaki Kiyono, S. Kougo, M. Takahashi, S. Motoike and T Niki. 1985. A travel consultation system: toward a smooth conversation in Japanese. In *Logic Programming '85: Proceedings of the 4th Conference, Tokyo*, Eiiti Wada, (ed.) Springer, Berlin, 226–235.

1545. Svartvik, Jan. 1980. Computer-aided grammatical tagging of spoken English. In *COLING-80*, 29–31.

1546. Swartout, Bill. 1982. GIST English generator. In *AAAI-82*, 404–409.

1547. Tait, John I. 1983. Semantic parsing and syntactic constraints (mark IV). In *Automatic Natural Language Parsing*, Karen Sparck-Jones and Yorick A. Wilks, (eds.) Ellis Horwood/Wiley, Chichester/New York, 169–177.

1548. Tait, John I. 1985. An English generator for a case-labelled dependency representation. In *ACL Proceedings, Second European Conference*, 194–197.

1549. Takeda, Koichi, Tetsunosuke Fujisaki and Emiko Suzuki. 1986. CRITAC-a Japanese text proofreading system. In *COLING-86*, 412–417.

1550. Tanaka, Hozumi. 1980. Unit-to unit interaction as a basis for semantic interpretation of Japanese sentences. In *COLING-80*, 383–388.

1551. Tanaka, Hozumi. 1986. DCKR - knowledge representation in PROLOG and its application to natural language processing. In *COLING-86*, 222–225.

1552. Tanaka, Takushi. 1980. Statistical analysis of Japanese characters. In *COLING-80*, 315–322.

1553. Tanaka, Yasuhito and Sho Yoshida. 1986. Acquisition of knowledge data by analyzing natural language. In *COLING-86*, 448–450.

1554. Tanenhaus, Michael K., Greg N. Carlson and Mark S Seidenberg. 1985. Do listeners compute linguistic representations?. In *Natural Language Parsing*, David R. Dowty, Lauri Karttunen and Arnold M. Zwicky, (eds.) Cambridge University Press, Cambridge, 359–408.

1555. Tannen, Deborah. 1980. The parameters of conversational style. In *ACL Proceedings, 18th Annual Meeting*, 39–40.

1556. Tazi, Said and Jacques Virbel. 1985. Formal representation of textual structures for an intelligent text-editing system. In *Natural Language Understanding and Logic Programming*, Veronica Dahl and Patrick Saint-Dizier, (eds.) North-Holland, Amsterdam, 191–205.

1557. Templeton, Marjorie and John Burger. 1983. Problems in natural language interface to DBMS with examples from EUFID. In *ACL Proceedings, Conference on Applied Natural Language Processing*, 3–16.

1558. Tennant, Harry R. 1981. What makes evaluation hard?. In *ACL Proceedings, 19th Annual Meeting*, 37–38.

1559. Tennant, Harry R. 1981. *Natural Language Processing*. Petrocelli, New York.

1560. Tennant, Harry R., Kenneth M. Ross, Richard M. Saenz, Craig W. Thompson and James R Miller. 1983. Menu-based natural language understanding. In *ACL Proceedings, 21st Annual Meeting*, 151–158.

1561. Tennant, Harry R. 1986. The commercial application of natural language interfaces. In *COLING-86*, 167.

1562. Teubert, Wolfgang. 1984. Applications of a lexicographical data base for German. In *COLING-84*, 34–37.

1563. Tešitelová, M. 1982. Quantification of meaning and the computer. In *COLING-82*, 377–382.

1564. Thibadeau, Robert, Marcel Just and Patricia Carpenter. 1980. Real Reading Behavior. In *ACL Proceedings, 18th Annual Meeting*, 159–162.

1565. Thomas, John. 1980. The computer as an active communication medium. In *ACL Proceedings, 18th Annual Meeting*, 83–86.

1566. Thomason, Richmond H. 1985. Accommodation, conversational planning, and implicature. In *Theoretical Approaches to Natural Language Understanding, a Workshop at Halifax, Nova Scotia*, 117–125.

1567. Thompson, Bozena Henisz. 1980. Linguistic analysis of natural language communication with computers. In *COLING-80*, 190–201.

1568. Thompson, Bozena Henisz. 1981. Evaluation of natural language interfaces to data base systems. In *ACL Proceedings, 19th Annual Meeting*, 39–42.

1569. Thompson, Bozena Henisz and Frederick B Thompson. 1983. Introducing ASK, a simple knowledgeable system. In *ACL Proceedings, Conference on Applied Natural Language Processing*, 17–24.

1570. Thompson, Frederick B. 1982. Solutions to issues depend on the Knowledge representation. In *ACL Proceedings, 20th Annual Meeting*, 169–171.

1571. Thompson, Henry S. 1981. Chart parsing and rule schemata in PSG. In *ACL Proceedings, 19th Annual Meeting*, 167–172.

1572. Thompson, Henry S. 1982. Handling metarules in a parser for GPSG. In *Developments in Generalized Phrase Structure Grammar*, Michael Barlow, Daniel P. Flickinger and Ivan A. Sag, (eds.) IULC, Bloomington, 26–37.

1573. Thompson, Henry S. 1983. Crossed serial dependencies: a low-power parsable extensions to GPSG. In *ACL Proceedings, 21st Annual Meeting*, 16–21.

1574. Thompson, Henry S. 1983. MCHART: a flexible, modular chart parsing system. In *AAAI-83*, 408–410.

1575. Thompson, Henry S. 1983. Natural language processing: a critical analysis of the structure of the field, with some implications for parsing. In *Automatic Natural Language Parsing*, Karen Sparck-Jones and Yorick A. Wilks, (eds.) Ellis Horwood/Wiley, Chichester/New York, 22–31.

1576. Thompson, Henry S. 1984. Speech transcription: an incremental, interactive approach. In *ECAI-84*, 697–704.

1577. Thompson, Henry S. and Graeme D Ritchie. 1984. Implementing natural language parsers. In *Artificial Intelligence: Tools, Techniques, and Applications*, Tim O'Shea and Marc Eisenstadt, (eds.) Harper & Row, New York, 245–300.

1578. Thompson, Henry S. 1985. Speech transcription: an incremental, interactive approach. In *Advances in Artificial Intelligence*, Tim O'Shea, (ed.) North-Holland, Amsterdam, 267–274.

1579. Thurmair, G. 1984. Linguistic problems in multilingual morphological decomposition. In *COLING-84*, 174–177.

1580. Tomabechi, Hideto. 1987. Direct memory access translation. *IJCAI-87* 2, 722–727.

1581. Tomita, Masaru. 1984. LR parsers for natural languages. In *COLING-84*, 354–357.

1582. Tomita, Masaru. 1984. Disambiguating grammatically ambiguous sentences by asking. In *COLING-84*, 476–480.

1583. Tomita, Masaru. 1985. An efficient context-free parsing algorithm for natural languages. *IJCAI-85* 2, 756–764.

1584. Tomita, Masaru and Jaime G Carbonell. 1986. Another stride towards knowledge-based machine translation. In *COLING-86*, 633–638.

1585. Tomita, Masaru. 1986. Sentence disambiguation by asking. *Computers and Translation* 1:1, 39–52.

1586. Tomita, Masaru. 1986. *Efficient Parsing for Natural Language: A Fast Algorithm for Practical Systems*. Kluwer, Boston.

1587. Tomita, Masaru and Jaime G Carbonell. 1987. The universal parser architecture for knowledge-based machine translation. *IJCAI-87* 2, 718–721.

1588. Tomita, Masaru. 1987. An efficient augmented context-free parsing algorithm. *Computational Linguistics* 13:1–2, 31–46.

1589. Torasso, Pietro, Leonardo Lesmo and Daniela Magnani. 1981. A deterministic analyzer for the interpretation of natural language commands. *IJCAI-81* 1, 440–442.

1590. Touretzky, David S. 1985. Inheritable relations: a logical extension to inheritance hierarchies. In *Theoretical Approaches to Natural Language Understanding, a Workshop at Halifax, Nova Scotia*, 55–60.

1591. Trivisonno, Giuseppe. 1982. Model for a legal semantic field: glossary of semantic subsets for legal automated documentation. In *Deontic Logic, Computational Linguistics and Legal Information Systems*, Antonio A. Martino, (ed.) North-Holland, Amsterdam, 339–348.

1592. Trost, Harald and Ernst Buchberger. 1986. Towards the automatic acquisition of lexical data. In *COLING-86*, 387–389.

1593. Tsujii, Jun-ichi. 1982. The transfer phase in an English-Japanese translation system. In *COLING-82*, 383–390.

1594. Tsujii, Jun-ichi, Jun-ichi Nakamura and Makoto Nagao. 1984. Analysis grammar of Japanese in the Mu-project - a procedural approach to analysis grammar. In *COLING-84*, 267–274.

1595. Tsujii, Jun-ichi. 1986. Future directions of machine translation. In *COLING-86*, 655–668.

1596. Tsurumaru, Hirosaki, Toru Hitaka and Sho Yoshida. 1986. An attempt to automatic thesaurus construction from an ordinary Japanese language dictionary. In *COLING-86*, 445–447.

1597. Tsutsumi, Taijiro. 1986. A prototype English-Japanese machine translation system for translating IBM computer manuals. In *COLING-86*, 646–648.

1598. Tucker, Allen B., Sergei Nirenburg and Victor Raskin. 1986. Discourse and cohesion in expository text. In *COLING-86*, 181–183.

1599. Tucker, Allen B. 1987. Current strategies in machine translation research. In *Machine Translation: Theoretical and Methodological Issues*, Sergei Nirenberg, (ed.) Cambridge University Press, Cambridge, 22–41.

1600. Turk, Christopher. 1984. A correction NL mechanism. In *ECAI-84*, 225–226.

1601. Turner, Raymond. 1987. Semantics in the lambda calculus. In *Proceedings of the Alvey Sponsored Workshop on Formal Semantics in Natural Language Processing*, Barry G.T. Lowden, (ed.) University of Essex, Colchester, 84–92.

1602. Turoff, Murray. 1980. Natural language and computer interface design. In *ACL Proceedings, 18th Annual Meeting*, 143–145.

1603. Tuttle, Mark S., David D. Sherertz, Marsden S. Blois and Stuart Nelson. 1983. Expertness from structured text? RECONSIDER: a diagnostic prompting program. In *ACL Proceedings, Conference on Applied Natural Language Processing*, 124–131.

1604. Uchida, Hiroshi and Kenji Sugiyama. 1980. A machine translation system from Japanese into English based on conceptual structure. In *COLING-80*, 455–462.

1605. Uchinami, Seiichi and Yoshikazu Tezuka. 1980. Linguistic model based on the generative topological information space. In *CO-LING-80*, 93–100.

1606. Uehara, Kuniaki, Ryo Ochitani, Osamu Mikami and Junichi Toyoda. 1984. Steps toward an actor-oriented integrated parser. In *Proceedings of the International Conference on Fifth Generation Computer Systems*, ICOT, Tokyo, 660–668.

1607. Uehara, Kuniaki, Ryo Ochitani, Osamu Kakusho and Junichi Toyoda. 1984. A bottom-up parser based on predicate logic: a survey of the formalism and its implementation technique. In *1984 International Symposium on Logic Programming*. IEEE Computer Society Press, Silver Spring, MD.

1608. Uehara, Kuniaki, Takashi Kakiuchi, Osamu Mikami and Junichi Toyoda. 1985. Extended PROLOG and its application to an integrated parser for text understanding. In *Logic Programming '85: Proceedings of the 4th Conference, Tokyo*, Eiiti Wada, (ed.) Springer, Berlin, 214–225.

1609. Uehara, Kuniaki, Ryo Ochitani, Osamu Mikami and Junichi Toyoda. 1985. An integrated parser for text understanding: viewing parsing as passing messages among actors. In *Natural Language Understanding and Logic Programming*, Veronica Dahl and Patrick Saint-Dizier, (eds.) North-Holland, Amsterdam, 79–95.

1610. Uemura, Syunsuke, Yasuo Sugawara, Mantaro J. Hashimoto and Akihiro Furuya. 1980. Automatic compilation of modern Chinese concordances. In *COLING-80*, 323–329.

1611. Uhlířová, L., I. Nebeská and J Kralik. 1982. Computational data analysis for syntax. In *COLING-82*, 391–396.

1612. Uszkoreit, Hans. 1983. A framework for processing partially free word order. In *ACL Proceedings, 21st Annual Meeting*, 106–112.

1613. Uszkoreit, Hans. 1986. Categorial unification grammar. In *CO-LING-86*, 187–194.

1614. Valkonen, K., Harri Jäppinen and Aarno Lehtola. 1987. Blackboard-based dependency parsing. *IJCAI-87* 2, 700–702.

1615. van Beek, Peter. 1987. A model for generating better explanations. In *ACL Proceedings, 25th Annual Meeting*, 215–220.

1616. van Eynde, Frank, Louis des Tombe and Fons Maes. 1985. The specification of time meaning for machine translation. In *ACL Proceedings, Second European Conference*, 35–40.

1617. Varile, N. 1983. Charts: a data structure for parsing. In *Parsing Natural Language*, Margaret King, (ed.) Academic Press, London, 73–87.

1618. Vasconcellos, Muriel. 1986. Functional considerations in the postediting of machine-translated output. *Computers and Translation* 1:1, 21–38.

1619. Vaughan, Marie M. and David D McDonald. 1986. The writing process as a model for natural language generation. In *ACL Proceedings, 24th Annual Meeting*, 90–96.

1620. Vauquois, Bernard and Christian Boitet. 1985. Automated translation at Grenoble University. *Computational Linguistics* 11:1, 28–36.

1621. Verastegui-Carvajal, J.N. 1982. Utilisation du parallelisme en traduction automatisée par ordinateur. In *COLING-82*, 397–405.

1622. Vergne, Jacques and Pascale Pagès. 1986. Synergy of syntax and morphology in automatic parsing of French language with a minimum of data. In *COLING-86*, 269–271.

1623. Veronis, Jean. 1987. Discourse consistency and many-sorted logic. *IJCAI-87* 2, 633–635.

1624. Vijay-Shanker, K., David J. Weir and Aravind K Joshi. 1986. Tree adjoining and head wrapping. In *COLING-86*, 202–207.

1625. Vijay-Shanker, K., David J. Weir and Aravind K Joshi. 1986. Adjoining, wrapping, and headed strings. In *ACL Proceedings, 24th Annual Meeting*, 67–74.

1626. Vijay-Shanker, K., David J. Weir and Aravind K Joshi. 1987. Characterizing structural descriptions produced by grammatical formalisms. In *ACL Proceedings, 25th Annual Meeting*, 104–111.

1627. Vilnat, Anne and Gérard Sabah. 1984. How a system may be self-conscious. In *ECAI-84*, 227–228.

1628. Vilnat, Anne and Gérard Sabah. 1985. Be brief, be to the point,... be seated or relevant responses in man/machine conversation. *IJCAI-85* 2, 852–854.

1629. Vladutz, George. 1983. Natural language text segmentation techniques applied to the automatic compilation of printed subject indexes and for online database access. In *ACL Proceedings, Conference on Applied Natural Language Processing*, 136–142.

1630. Wachtel, Tom. 1986. Pragmatic sensitivity in NL interfaces and the structure of conversation. In *COLING-86*, 35–41.

1631. Wada, Hajime and Nicholas Asher. 1986. BUILDRS: an implementation of DR theory and LFG. In *COLING-86*, 540–545.

1632. Wahlster, Wolfgang. 1980. Towards a computational model for the semantics of why-questions. In *COLING-80*, 144–150.

1633. Wahlster, Wolfgang, Heinz Marburger, Anthony Jameson and Stephan Busemann. 1983. Over-answering yes-no questions: extended responses in a NL interface to a vision system. In *IJCAI-83*, 643–646.

1634. Wahlster, Wolfgang. 1986. Natural language interfaces - ready for commercial success ?. In *COLING-86*, 161.

1635. Walker, Donald E. 1982. Natural-language-access systems and the organization and use of information. In *COLING-82*, 407–412.

1636. Walker, Donald E. 1982. Reflections on 20 years of the ACL: an introduction. In *ACL Proceedings, 20th Annual Meeting*, 89–91.

1637. Walker, Donald E. 1982. A society in transition. In *ACL Proceedings, 20th Annual Meeting*, 98–99.

1638. Walker, Donald E. 1983. Text analysis. In *ACL Proceedings, Conference on Applied Natural Language Processing*, 107–108.

1639. Walker, Donald E. 1984. Machine-readable dictionaries. In *COLING-84*, 457.

1640. Walker, Donald E. 1987. Knowledge resource tools for accessing large text files. In *Machine Translation: Theoretical and Methodological Issues*, Sergei Nirenberg, (ed.) Cambridge University Press, Cambridge, 247–261.

1641. Wallace, Mark. 1984. *Communicating with Databases in Natural Language*. Ellis Horwood/Wiley, Chichester/New York.

1642. Waltz, David L. 1980. Understanding scene descriptions as event simulations. In *ACL Proceedings, 18th Annual Meeting*, 7–11.

1643. Waltz, David L. 1981. Generating and understanding scene descriptions. In *Elements of Discourse Understanding*, Aravind K. Joshi, Bonnie Lynn Webber and Ivan Sag, (eds.) Cambridge University Press, Cambridge, 266–282.

1644. Waltz, David L. 1981. Toward a detailed model of processing for language describing the physical world. *IJCAI-81* 1, 1–6.

1645. Waltz, David L. 1982. Event shape diagrams. In *AAAI-82*, 84–87.

1646. Waltz, David L. 1982. The state of the art in natural-language understanding. In *Strategies for Natural Language Processing*, Wendy G. Lehnert and Martin H. Ringle, (eds.) Erlbaum, Hillsdale, 3–32.

1647. Waltz, David L. and Jordan B Pollack. 1984. Massively parallel parsing: a strongly interactive model of natural language interpretation. *Cognitive Science* 9:1, 51–74.

1648. Waltz, David L. 1986. Connectionist models for natural language processing. In *ACL Proceedings, 24th Annual Meeting*, 185.

1649. Waltz, David L. 1987. Connectionist models: not just a notational variant, not a panacea. In *TINLAP-3*, 56–62.

1650. Wang, Juen-tin. 1980. On computational sentence generation from logical form. In *COLING-80*, 405–411.

1651. Wanner, Eric. 1980. The ATN and the sausage machine: which one is baloney. *Cognition* 8, 209–226.

1652. Warotamasikkhadit, Udom. 1986. Computer aided translation project, University Sains Malaysia, Penang, Malaysia. *Computers and Translation* 1:2, 113–114.

1653. Warren, David H.D. 1982. Issues in natural language access to databases from a logic programming perspective. In *ACL Proceedings, 20th Annual Meeting*, 63–66.

1654. Warren, David H.D. and Fernando C.N Pereira. 1982. An efficient easily adaptable system for interpreting natural language queries. *American Journal of Computational Linguistics* 8:3–4, 110–122.

1655. Warren, David S. and Joyce Friedman. 1982. Using semantics in non-context-free parsing of Montague grammar. *American Journal of Computational Linguistics* 8:3–4, 123–138.

1656. Warren, David S. 1983. Using lambda-calculus to represent meanings in logic grammars. In *.cx*, 51–56.

1657. Warren, David S. 1985. Using Montague semantics in natural language understanding. In *Theoretical Approaches to Natural Language Understanding, a Workshop at Halifax, Nova Scotia*, 61–68.

1658. Wasserman, Kenneth. 1985. A survey of programs for semantic-based natural language processing. *The AI Magazine* 5:4, 28–42.

1659. Webber, Bonnie Lynn. 1986 (1983). So what can we talk about now?. In *Readings in Natural Language Processing*, Barbara J. Grosz, Karen Sparck-Jones and Bonnie Lynn Webber, (eds.) Morgan Kaufmann, Los Altos, 395–414.

1660. Webber, Bonnie Lynn. 1980. Interactive discourse: looking to the future. In *ACL Proceedings, 18th Annual Meeting*, 127.

1661. Webber, Bonnie Lynn. 1980. *A Formal Approach to Discourse Anaphora*. Garland, New York.

1662. Webber, Bonnie Lynn. 1981. Discourse model synthesis: preliminaries to reference. In *Elements of Discourse Understanding*, Aravind K. Joshi, Bonnie Lynn Webber and Ivan Sag, (eds.) Cambridge University Press, Cambridge, 283–299.

1663. Webber, Bonnie Lynn and Aravind K Joshi. 1982. Taking the initiative in natural language data base interactions: justifying why. In *COLING-82*, 413–419.

1664. Webber, Bonnie Lynn and Timothy W Finin. 1982. *Natural Language Interfaces I: Basic Theory and Practice*. AAAI, Menlo Park.

1665. Webber, Bonnie Lynn and Eric Mays. 1983. Varieties of user misconceptions: detection and correction. In *IJCAI-83*, 650–652.

1666. Webber, Bonnie Lynn, Aravind K. Joshi, Eric Mays and Kathleen R McKeown. 1983. Extended natural language data base interactions. *Computers and Mathematics with Applications* 9:1, 233-244.

1667. Webber, Bonnie Lynn. 1983. So what can we talk about now?. In *Computational Models of Discourse*, Michael Brady and Robert C. Berwick, (eds.) MIT Press, Cambridge, Ma., 331-371.

1668. Webber, Bonnie Lynn. 1987. Position paper: event reference. In *TINLAP-3*, 137-142.

1669. Webber, Bonnie Lynn. 1987. The interpretation of tense in discourse. In *ACL Proceedings, 25th Annual Meeting*, 147-154.

1670. Webber, David J. and William C Mann. 1981. Prospects for computer-assisted dialect adaptation. *American Journal of Computational Linguistics* 7:3, 165-177.

1671. Webber, Howard R. 1984. Machine-readable components in a variety of information-system applications. In *COLING-84*, 463.

1672. Wedekind, Jürgen. 1986. A concept derivation for LFG. In *COLING-86*, 487-489.

1673. Wehrli, Eric. 1983. A modular parser for French. In *IJCAI-83*, 686-689.

1674. Wehrli, Eric. 1985. Design and implementation of a lexical data base. In *ACL Proceedings, Second European Conference*, 146-153.

1675. Weiner, James L. 1980. BLAH, A system which explains its reasoning. *Artificial Intelligence* 15:1,2, 19-48.

1676. Weiner, Judith E. 1984. A knowledge representation approach to understanding metaphors. *Computational Linguistics* 10:1, 1-14.

1677. Weischedel, Ralph M. Mapping between semantic representations using Horn clauses. In *AAAI-83*, 424-428.

1678. Weischedel, Ralph M. 1986 (1979). A new semantic computation while parsing: presupposition and entailment. In *Readings in Natural Language Processing*, Barbara J. Grosz, Karen Sparck-Jones and Bonnie Lynn Webber, (eds.) Morgan Kaufmann, Los Altos, 313-326.

1679. Weischedel, Ralph M. and John E Black. 1980. If the parser fails. In *ACL Proceedings, 18th Annual Meeting*, 95-96.

1680. Weischedel, Ralph M. and John E Black. 1980. Responding intelligently to unparsable inputs. *American Journal of Computational Linguistics* 6:2, 87-109.

1681. Weischedel, Ralph M. and Norman K Sondheimer. 1982. An improved heuristic for ellipsis processing. In *ACL Proceedings, 20th Annual Meeting*, 85-88.

1682. Weischedel, Ralph M. and Norman K Sondheimer. 1983. Meta-rules as a basis for processing ill-formed output. *American Journal of Computational Linguistics* 9:3–4, 161–177.

1683. Weischedel, Ralph M. 1983. Handling ill-formed input. In *ACL Proceedings, Conference on Applied Natural Language Processing*, 89–92.

1684. Weischedel, Ralph M. and Lance A Ramshaw. 1987. Reflections on the knowledge needed to parse ill-formed language. In *Machine Translation: Theoretical and Methodological Issues*, Sergei Nirenberg, (ed.) Cambridge University Press, Cambridge, 155–167.

1685. White, John S. 1986. What should machine translation be?. In *ACL Proceedings, 24th Annual Meeting*, 267.

1686. White, John S. 1987. The research environment in the Metal project. In *Machine Translation: Theoretical and Methodological Issues*, Sergei Nirenberg, (ed.) Cambridge University Press, Cambridge, 225–246.

1687. Whitelock, Peter J., Mary McGee Wood, Brian J. Chandler, Natsuko Holden and Heather J Horsfall. 1986. Strategies for interactive machine translation: the experience and implications of the UMIST Japanese project. In *COLING-86*, 329–334.

1688. Wiese, Richard. 1986. The role of phonology in speech processing. In *COLING-86*, 608–611.

1689. Wilensky, Robert. 1986 (1982). Points: a theory of the structure of stories in memory. In *Readings in Natural Language Processing*, Barbara J. Grosz, Karen Sparck-Jones and Bonnie Lynn Webber, (eds.) Morgan Kaufmann, Los Altos, 459–473.

1690. Wilensky, Robert and Yigal Arens. 1980. PHRAN - a knowledge based natural language understander. In *ACL Proceedings, 18th Annual Meeting*, 117–121.

1691. Wilensky, Robert. 1980. What's the point ?. In *Proceedings of the Third Biennial Conference of the Canadian Society for Computational Studies of Intelligence (3rd Canadian Conference on AI)*, 256–262.

1692. Wilensky, Robert. 1981. Meta-planning: representing and using knowledge about planning in problem solving and natural language understanding. *Cognitive Science* 5:3, 197–235.

1693. Wilensky, Robert. 1981. PAM. In *Inside Computer Understanding: Five Programs plus Miniatures*, Roger C. Schank and Christopher K. Riesbeck, (eds.) Erlbaum, Hillsdale, 136–179.

1694. Wilensky, Robert. 1981. Micro PAM. In *Inside Computer Understanding: Five Programs plus Miniatures*, Roger C. Schank and Christopher K. Riesbeck, (eds.) Erlbaum, Hillsdale, 180–196.

1695. Wilensky, Robert. 1981. A knowledge-based approach to language processing; a progress report. *IJCAI-81* 1, 25–30.

1696. Wilensky, Robert. 1982. Points: a theory of the structure of stories in memory. In *Strategies for Natural Language Processing*, Wendy G. Lehnert and Martin H. Ringle, (eds.) Erlbaum, Hillsdale, 345–374.

1697. Wilensky, Robert. 1982. Talking to UNIX in English: an overview of UC. In *AAAI-82*, 103–106.

1698. Wilensky, Robert. 1983. *Planning and understanding.* Addison Wesley, New York.

1699. Wilensky, Robert. 1987. Some complexities of goal analysis. In *TINLAP-3*, 97–99.

1700. Wilks, Yorick A. 1986 (1975). An intelligent analyzer and understander of English. In *Readings in Natural Language Processing*, Barbara J. Grosz, Karen Sparck-Jones and Bonnie Lynn Webber, (eds.) Morgan Kaufmann, Los Altos, 193–203.

1701. Wilks, Yorick A. 1981. A position note on natural language understanding and artificial intelligence. *Cognition* 10, 337–340.

1702. Wilks, Yorick A. 1982. Discussion of Roger C. Schank's paper. In *Text Processing: Text Analysis and Generation, Text Typology and Attribution*, Sture Allén, (ed.) Almqvist and Wiksell, Stockholm, 65–74.

1703. Wilks, Yorick A. 1982. Some thoughts on procedural semantics. In *Strategies for Natural Language Processing*, Wendy G. Lehnert and Martin H. Ringle, (eds.) Erlbaum, Hillsdale, 495–516.

1704. Wilks, Yorick A. 1983. Machine translation and the artificial intelligence paradigm of language processes. In *Computers in Language Research 2*, Walter A. Sedelow Jr. and Sally Yeates Sedelow, (eds.) Trends in Linguistics, Walter de Gruyter & Co., Berlin, 61–111.

1705. Wilks, Yorick A. 1983. Deep and superficial parsing. In *Parsing Natural Language*, Margaret King, (ed.) Academic Press, London, 219–246.

1706. Wilks, Yorick A. and Karen Sparck-Jones. 1983. Introduction: a little light history. In *Automatic Natural Language Parsing*, Karen Sparck-Jones and Yorick A. Wilks, (eds.) Ellis Horwood/Wiley, Chichester/New York, 11–21.

1707. Wilks, Yorick A. 1983. Does anyone really still believe this kind of thing?. In *Automatic Natural Language Parsing*, Karen Sparck-Jones and Yorick A. Wilks, (eds.) Ellis Horwood/Wiley, Chichester/New York, 182–189.

1708. Wilks, Yorick A. 1985. Right attachment and preference semantics. In *ACL Proceedings, Second European Conference*, 89–92.

1709. Wilks, Yorick A., Xiuming Huang and Dan Fass. 1985. Syntax, preference and right attachment. *IJCAI-85* 2, 779–784.

1710. Wilks, Yorick A. 1987. On keeping logic in its place. In *TINLAP-3*, 110–114.

1711. Winograd, Terry. 1986 (1973). A procedural model of language and understanding. In *Readings in Natural Language Processing*, Barbara J. Grosz, Karen Sparck-Jones and Bonnie Lynn Webber, (eds.) Morgan Kaufmann, Los Altos, 249–266.

1712. Winograd, Terry. 1983. *Language as a Cognitive Process: Syntax.* Addison-Wesley., Reading, Ma..

1713. Witten, Ian H. 1980. Translating interactive computer dialogues from ideographic to alphabetic languages. In *COLING-80*, 526–533.

1714. Wittenburg, Kent. 1986. A parser for portable ML interfaces using graph-unification-based grammars. *AAAI-86* 2, 1053–1058.

1715. Wittenburg, Kent. 1987. Predictive combinators: a method for efficient processing of combinatory categorial grammars. In *ACL Proceedings, 25th Annual Meeting*, 73–80.

1716. Wolff, J. Gerard. 1980. Language acquisition and the discovery of phrase structure. *Language and Speech* 23, 255–269.

1717. Wolff, J. Gerard. 1980. Data compression, generalisation and over-generalisation in an evolving theory of language development. In *AISB-80*, 298–307.

1718. Wolff, J. Gerard. 1982. Language acquisition, data compression and generalization. *Language and Communication* 2, 57–89.

1719. Wolff, J. Gerard. 1984. Cognitive development as optimisation. In *Knowledge Based Learning Systems*, Leonard Bolc, (ed.) Springer, Berlin, 00–00.

1720. Wong, Douglas. 1981. Language comprehension in a problem solver. *IJCAI-81* 1, 7–12.

1721. Woods, William A. 1986 (1970). Transition network grammars for natural language analysis. In *Readings in Natural Language Processing*, Barbara J. Grosz, Karen Sparck-Jones and Bonnie Lynn Webber, (eds.) Morgan Kaufmann, Los Altos, 71–87.

1722. Woods, William A. 1986 (1978). Semantics and quantification in natural language question answering. In *Readings in Natural Language Processing*, Barbara J. Grosz, Karen Sparck-Jones and Bonnie Lynn Webber, (eds.) Morgan Kaufmann, Los Altos, 205–248.

1723. Woods, William A. 1980. Cascaded ATN grammars. *American Journal of Computational Linguistics* 6:1, 1–12.

1724. Woods, William A. 1981. Procedural semantics as a theory of meaning. In *Elements of Discourse Understanding*, Aravind K. Joshi, Bonnie Lynn Webber and Ivan Sag, (eds.) Cambridge University Press, Cambridge, 300–334.

1725. Woods, William A. 1981. Optimal search strategies for speech-understanding control. In *Readings in Artificial Intelligence*, Bonnie Lynn Webber and Nils J. Nilsson, (eds.) Tioga, Palo Alto, 30–68.

1726. Woods, William A. 1982. Optimal search strategies for speech understanding control. *Artificial Intelligence* 18:3, 295–326.

1727. Wothke, Klaus. 1986. Machine learning of morphological rules by generalization and analogy. In *COLING-86*, 289–293.

1728. Wroblewski, David. 1987. Nondestructive graph unificatio. In *AAAI-87*, 582–589.

1729. Wynn, Eleanor. 1980. What discourse aren't needed in online dialogue. In *ACL Proceedings, 18th Annual Meeting*, 87–90.

1730. Xinsong, Jiang, Li Yingtan and Chen Yu. 1984. Understanding the Chinese language. In *Computational Models of Natural Language Processing*, Bruno G. Bara and Giovanni Guida, (eds.) North-Holland, Amsterdam, 197–225.

1731. Yamada, Sae. 1983. Iterative operations. In *ACL Proceedings, First European Conference*, 14–20.

1732. Yamauchi, Hiroyuki. 1980. Processing of syntax and semantics of natural language by predicate logic. In *COLING-80*, 389–396.

1733. Yan, Yongfeng. 1986. Structural correspondence specification environment. In *COLING-86*, 81–84.

1734. Yang, C.J. 1981. High level memory structures and text coherence in translation. *IJCAI-81* 1, 47–48.

1735. Yang, Yiming and Toyoaki Nishida. 1984. Use of heuristic knowledge in Chinese language analysis. In *COLING-84*, 222–225.

1736. Yang, Yiming, Shuji Doshita and Toyoaki Nishida. 1985. Partial constraints in Chinese analysis. *IJCAI-85* 2, 826–828.

1737. Yang, Yiming. 1987. Semantic analysis in Chinese sentence analysis. *IJCAI-87* 2, 679–681.

1738. Yasukawa, Hideki. 1984. LFG system in PROLOG. In *COLING-84*, 358–361.

1739. Yazdani, Masoud. 1982. How to write a story. In *ECAI-82*, 259–260.

1740. Yegnanarayana, B., J.M. Naik and D.G Childers. 1984. Voice simulation: factors affecting quality and naturalness. In *COLING-84*, 530–533.

1741. Yip, Kenneth Man-Kam. 1985. Tense, aspect, and cognitive representation of time. *IJCAI-85* 2, 806–814.

1742. Yip, Kenneth Man-Kam. 1985. Tense, aspect and the cognitive representation of time. In *ACL Proceedings, 23rd Annual Meeting*, 18–26.

1743. Yngve, Victor H. 1982. Our Double Anniversary. In *ACL Proceedings, 20th Annual Meeting*, 92–94.

1744. Yokoi, Toshio, Kuniaki Mukai, Hideo Miyoshi, Yuichi Tanaka and Ryoichi Sugimura. 1986. Research activities on natural language processing of the FGCS project. *ICOT Journal* 14, 1–8.

1745. Yokoyama, Shoichi and Kenji Hanakata. 1986. Conceptual lexicon using an object-oriented language. In *COLING-86*, 226–228.

1746. Yonezaki, Naoki and Hajime Enomoto. 1980. Database system based on intensional logic. In *COLING-80*, 220–227.

1747. Yoshida, Sho, Hirosaki Tsurumaru and Toru Hitaka. 1982. Man-assisted machine construction of a semantic dictionary for natural language processing. In *COLING-82*, 419–424.

1748. Yoshida, Sho. 1984. A consideration on the concepts structure and language in relation to selections of translation equivalents of verbs in machine translation systems. In *COLING-84*, 167–169.

1749. Yoshii, Rika. 1987. JETR: a robust machine translation system. In *ACL Proceedings, 25th Annual Meeting*, 25–31.

1750. Yusoff, Zaharin. 1986. Strategies and heuristics in the analysis of a natural language in machine translation. In *COLING-86*, 136–139.

1751. Zadeh, Lotfi A. 1982. Test-score semantics for natural languages. In *COLING-82*, 425–430.

1752. Zadeh, Lotfi A. 1983. A computational approach to fuzzy quantifiers in natural language. *Computers and Mathematics with Applications* 9:1, 149–184.

1753. Zadeh, Lotfi A. 1984. A computational theory of dispositions. In *COLING-84*, 312–318.

1754. Zajac, Rémi. 1986. SCSL: a linguistic specification language for MT. In *COLING-86*, 393–398.

1755. Zarechnak, Michael. 1986. The intermediary language for multi-language translation. *Computers and Translation* 1:2, 83–92.

1756. Zarri, Gian Piero. 1983. Automatic representation of the semantic relationships corresponding to a French surface expression. In *ACL Proceedings, Conference on Applied Natural Language Processing*, 143–147.

1757. Zelinsky-Wibbelt, Cornelia. 1986. An empirically based approach towards a system of semantic features. In *COLING-86*, 7–12.

1758. Zernick, Uri and Michael G Dyer. 1985. Towards a self-extending lexicon. In *ACL Proceedings, 23rd Annual Meeting*, 284–292.

1759. Zernik, Uri and Michael G Dyer. 1986. Disambiguation and language acquisition through the phrasal lexicon. In *COLING-86*, 247–252.

1760. Zifonun, G. 1980. Levels of representation in natural language based information systems and their relation to the methodology of computational linguistics. In *COLING-80*, 202–208.

1761. Zimmermann, Harald H. 1980. Natürlichsprachige Problembeschreibung als ein Verfahren für den bürgernahen Zugang zu Dokumentationssystemen. In *COLING-80*, 558.

1762. Zock, Michael, Gérard Sabah and Christophe Alviset. 1986. From structure to process: computer-assisted teaching of various strategies for generating pronoun constructions in French. In *COLING-86*, 566–569.

1763. Zoeppritz, Magdalena. 1981. The meaning of 'of' and 'have' in the USL system. *American Journal of Computational Linguistics* 7:2, 109–119.

1764. Zukerman, Ingrid and Judea Perl. 1986. Comprehension-driven generation of meta-technical utterances in math tutoring. *AAAI-86* 1, 606–611.

Index to Keywords

121

Index to Second
and Subsequent Authors

CSLI Publications

Reports

The following titles have been published in the CSLI Reports series. These reports may be obtained from CSLI Publications, Ventura Hall, Stanford University, Stanford, CA 94305.

The Situation in Logic–I. Jon Barwise. CSLI–84–2. ($2.00)

Coordination and How to Distinguish Categories. Ivan Sag, Gerald Gazdar, Thomas Wasow, and Steven Weisler. CSLI–84–3. ($3.50)

Belief and Incompleteness. Kurt Konolige. CSLI–84–4. ($4.50)

Equality, Types, Modules and Generics for Logic Programming. Joseph Goguen and José Meseguer. CSLI–84–5. ($2.50)

Lessons from Bolzano. Johan van Benthem. CSLI–84–6. ($1.50)

Self-propagating Search: A Unified Theory of Memory. Pentti Kanerva. CSLI–84–7. ($9.00)

Reflection and Semantics in LISP. Brian Cantwell Smith. CSLI–84–8. ($2.50)

The Implementation of Procedurally Reflective Languages. Jim des Rivières and Brian Cantwell Smith. CSLI–84–9. ($3.00)

Parameterized Programming. Joseph Goguen. CSLI–84–10. ($3.50)

Morphological Constraints on Scandinavian Tone Accent. Meg Withgott and Per-Kristian Halvorsen. CSLI–84–11. ($2.50)

Partiality and Nonmonotonicity in Classical Logic. Johan van Benthem. CSLI–84–12. ($2.00)

Shifting Situations and Shaken Attitudes. Jon Barwise and John Perry. CSLI–84–13. ($4.50)

Aspectual Classes in Situation Semantics. Robin Cooper. CSLI–85–14–C. ($4.00)

Completeness of Many-Sorted Equational Logic. Joseph Goguen and José Meseguer. CSLI–84–15. ($2.50)

Moving the Semantic Fulcrum. Terry Winograd. CSLI–84–17. ($1.50)

On the Mathematical Properties of Linguistic Theories. C. Raymond Perrault. CSLI–84–18. ($3.00)

A Simple and Efficient Implementation of Higher-order Functions in LISP. Michael P. Georgeff and Stephen F.Bodnar. CSLI–84–19. ($4.50)

On the Axiomatization of "if-then-else". Irène Guessarian and José Meseguer. CSLI–85–20. ($3.00)

The Situation in Logic–II: Conditionals and Conditional Information. Jon Barwise. CSLI–84–21. ($3.00)

Principles of OBJ2. Kokichi Futatsugi, Joseph A. Goguen, Jean-Pierre Jouannaud, and José Meseguer. CSLI–85–22. ($2.00)

Querying Logical Databases. Moshe Vardi. CSLI–85–23. ($1.50)

Computationally Relevant Properties of Natural Languages and Their Grammar. Gerald Gazdar and Geoff Pullum. CSLI–85–24. ($3.50)

An Internal Semantics for Modal Logic: Preliminary Report. Ronald Fagin and Moshe Vardi. CSLI–85–25. ($2.00)

The Situation in Logic–III: Situations, Sets and the Axiom of Foundation. Jon Barwise. CSLI–85–26. ($2.50)

Semantic Automata. Johan van Benthem. CSLI–85–27. ($2.50)

Restrictive and Non-Restrictive Modification. Peter Sells. CSLI–85–28. ($3.00)

238

Institutions: Abstract Model Theory for Computer Science. J. A. Goguen and R. M. Burstall. CSLI-85-30. ($4.50)

A Formal Theory of Knowledge and Action. Robert C. Moore. CSLI-85-31. ($5.50)

Finite State Morphology: A Review of Koskenniemi (1983). Gerald Gazdar. CSLI-85-32. ($1.50)

The Role of Logic in Artificial Intelligence. Robert C. Moore. CSLI-85-33. ($2.00)

Applicability of Indexed Grammars to Natural Languages. Gerald Gazdar. CSLI-85-34. ($2.00)

Commonsense Summer: Final Report. Jerry R. Hobbs, et al.. CSLI-85-35. ($12.00)

Limits of Correctness in Computers. Brian Cantwell Smith. CSLI-85-36. ($2.50)

On the Coherence and Structure of Discourse. Jerry R. Hobbs. CSLI-85-37. ($3.00)

The Coherence of Incoherent Discourse. Jerry R. Hobbs and Michael H. Agar. CSLI-85-38. ($2.50)

The Structures of Discourse Structure. Barbara Grosz and Candace L. Sidner. CSLI-85-39. ($4.50)

A Complete Type-free, Second-order Logic and its Philosophical Foundations. Christopher Menzel. CSLI-86-40. ($4.50)

Possible-world Semantics for Autoepistemic Logic. Robert C. Moore. CSLI-85-41. ($2.00)

Deduction with Many-Sorted Rewrite. José Meseguer and Joseph A. Goguen. CSLI-85-42. ($1.50)

On Some Formal Properties of Metarules. Hans Uszkoreit and Stanley Peters. CSLI-85-43. ($1.50)

Language, Mind, and Information. John Perry. CSLI-85-44. ($2.00)

Constraints on Order. Hans Uszkoreit. CSLI-86-46. ($3.00)

Linear Precedence in Discontinuous Constituents: Complex Fronting in German. Hans Uszkoreit. CSLI-86-47. ($2.50)

A Compilation of Papers on Unification-Based Grammar Formalisms, Parts I and II. Stuart M. Shieber, Fernando C.N. Pereira, Lauri Karttunen, and Martin Kay. CSLI-86-48. ($4.00)

An Algorithm for Generating Quantifier Scopings. Jerry R. Hobbs and Stuart M. Shieber. CSLI-86-49. ($2.50)

Verbs of Change, Causation, and Time. Dorit Abusch. CSLI-86-50. ($2.00)

Noun-Phrase Interpretation. Mats Rooth. CSLI-86-51. ($2.50)

Noun Phrases, Generalized Quantifiers and Anaphora. Jon Barwise. CSLI-86-52. ($2.50)

Circumstantial Attitudes and Benevolent Cognition. John Perry. CSLI-86-53. ($1.50)

A Study in the Foundations of Programming Methodology: Specifications, Institutions, Charters and Parchments. Joseph A. Goguen and R. M. Burstall. CSLI-86-54. ($2.50)

Quantifiers in Formal and Natural Languages. Dag Westerståhl. CSLI-86-55. ($7.50)

Intentionality, Information, and Matter. Ivan Blair. CSLI-86-56. ($3.00)

Graphs and Grammars. William Marsh. CSLI-86-57. ($2.00)

Computer Aids for Comparative Dictionaries. Mark Johnson. CSLI-86-58. ($2.00)

The Relevance of Computational Linguistics. Lauri Karttunen. CSLI-86-59. ($2.50)

Grammatical Hierarchy and Linear Precedence. Ivan A. Sag. CSLI-86-60. ($3.50)

D-PATR: A Development Environment for Unification-Based Grammars. Lauri Karttunen. CSLI-86-61. ($4.00)

A Sheaf-Theoretic Model of Concurrency. Luís F. Monteiro and Fernando C. N. Pereira. CSLI-86-62. ($3.00)

Discourse, Anaphora and Parsing. Mark Johnson. CSLI–86–63. (*$2.00*)

Tarski on Truth and Logical Consequence. John Etchemendy. CSLI–86–64. (*$3.50*)

The LFG Treatment of Discontinuity and The Double Infinitive Construction in Dutch. Mark Johnson. CSLI–86–65. (*$2.50*)

Categorial Unification Grammars. Hans Uszkoreit. CSLI–86–66. (*$2.50*)

Generalized Quantifiers and Plurals. Godehard Link. CSLI–86–67. (*$2.00*)

Radical Lexicalism. Lauri Karttunen. CSLI–86–68. (*$2.50*)

Understanding Computers and Cognition: Four Reviews and a Response. Mark Stefik, Editor. CSLI–87–70. (*$3.50*)

The Corresponding Continuum. Brian Cantwell Smith. CSLI–87–71. (*$4.00*)

The Role of Propositional Objects of Belief in Action. David J. Israel. CSLI–87–72. (*$2.50*)

From Worlds to Situations. John Perry. CSLI–87–73. (*$2.00*)

Two Replies. Jon Barwise. CSLI–87–74. (*$3.00*)

Semantics of Clocks. Brian Cantwell Smith. CSLI–87–75. (*$3.50*)

Varieties of Self-Reference. Brian Cantwell Smith. CSLI–87–76. (*Forthcoming*)

The Parts of Perception. Alexander Pentland. CSLI–87–77. (*$4.00*)

Topic, Pronoun, and Agreement in Chicheŵa. Joan Bresnan and S. A. Mchombo. CSLI–87–78. (*$5.00*)

HPSG: An Informal Synopsis. Carl Pollard and Ivan A. Sag. CSLI–87–79. (*$4.50*)

The Situated Processing of Situated Languages. Susan Stucky. CSLI–87–80. (*$1.50*)

Muir: A Tool for Language Design. Terry Winograd. CSLI–87–81. (*$2.50*)

Final Algebras, Cosemicomputable Algebras, and Degrees of Unsolvability. Lawrence S. Moss, José Meseguer, and Joseph A. Goguen. CSLI–87–82. (*$3.00*)

The Synthesis of Digital Machines with Provable Epistemic Properties. Stanley J. Rosenschein and Leslie Pack Kaelbling. CSLI–87–83. (*$3.50*)

Formal Theories of Knowledge in AI and Robotics. Stanley J. Rosenschein. CSLI–87–84. (*$1.50*)

An Architecture for Intelligent Reactive Systems. Leslie Pack Kaelbling. CSLI–87–85. (*$2.00*)

Order-Sorted Unification. José Meseguer, Joseph A. Goguen, and Gert Smolka. CSLI–87–86. (*$2.50*)

Modular Algebraic Specification of Some Basic Geometrical Constructions. Joseph A. Goguen. CSLI–87–87. (*$2.50*)

Persistence, Intention and Commitment. Phil Cohen and Hector Levesque. CSLI–87–88. (*$3.50*)

Rational Interaction as the Basis for Communication. Phil Cohen and Hector Levesque. CSLI–87–89. (*$3.50*)

An Application of Default Logic to Speech Act Theory. C. Raymond Perrault. CSLI–87–90. (*$2.50*)

Models and Equality for Logical Programming. Joseph A. Goguen and José Meseguer. CSLI–87–91. (*$3.00*)

Order-Sorted Algebra Solves the Constructor-Selector, Multiple Representation and Coercion Problems. Joseph A. Goguen and José Meseguer. CSLI–87–92. (*$2.00*)

Extensions and Foundations for Object-Oriented Programming. Joseph A. Goguen and José Meseguer. CSLI–87–93. (*$3.50*)

L3 Reference Manual: Version 2.19. William Poser. CSLI–87–94. (*$2.50*)

Change, Process and Events. Carol E. Cleland. CSLI–87–95. (*Forthcoming*)

One, None, a Hundred Thousand Specification Languages. Joseph A. Goguen CSLI–87–96. (*$2.00*)

Constituent Coordination in HPSG Derek Proudian and David Goddeau CSLI–87–97. (*$2.00*)

A Language/Action Perspective on the Design of Cooperative Work Terry Winograd CSLI–87–98. (*$3.00*)

Implicature and Definite Reference Jerry R. Hobbs CSLI–87–99. (*$1.50*)

Thinking Machines: Can There be? Are we? Terry Winograd CSLI–87–100. (*$2.50*)

Situation Semantics and Semantic Interpretation in Constraint-Based Grammars Per-Kristian Halvorsen CSLI–87–101. (*$1.50*)

Category Structures Gerald Gazdar, Geoffrey K. Pullum, Robert Carpenter, Ewan Klein, Thomas E. Hukari, Robert D. Levine CSLI–87–102. (*$3.00*)

Cognitive Theories of Emotion Ronald Alan Nash CSLI–87–103. (*$2.50*)

Toward an Architecture for Resource-Bounded Agents Martha E. Pollack, David J. Israel, and Michael E. Bratman CSLI–87–104. (*$2.00*)

On the Relation Between Default and Autoepistemic Logic Kurt Konolige CSLI–87–105. (*$3.00*)

Three Responses to Situation Theory Terry Winograd CSLI–87–106. (*$2.50*)

Subjects and Complements in HPSG Robert Borsley CSLI–87–107. (*$2.50*)

Tools for Morphological Analysis Mary Dalrymple, Ronald M. Kaplan, Lauri Karttunen, Kimmo Koskenniemi, Sami Shaio, Michael Wescoat CSLI–87–108. (*$10.00*)

Fourth Year Report of the Situated Language Research Program CSLI–87–111. (*Forthcoming*)

Bare Plurals, Naked Relatives, and Their Kin Dietmar Zaefferer CSLI–87–112. (*Forthcoming*)

Lecture Notes

The titles in this series are distributed by the University of Chicago Press and may be purchased in academic or university bookstores or ordered directly from the distributor at 5801 Ellis Avenue, Chicago, Illinois 60637.

A Manual of Intensional Logic. Johan van Benthem. Lecture Notes No. 1.

Emotion and Focus. Helen Fay Nissenbaum. Lecture Notes No. 2.

Lectures on Contemporary Syntactic Theories. Peter Sells with a Postscript by Thomas Wasow. Lecture Notes No. 3.

An Introduction to Unification-Based Approaches to Grammar. Stuart M. Shieber. Lecture Notes No. 4.

The Semantics of Destructive LISP. Ian A. Mason. Lecture Notes No. 5.

An Essay on Facts. Kenneth Russell Olson. Lecture Notes No. 6.

Logics of Time and Computation. Robert Goldblatt. Lecture Notes No. 7.

Word Order and Constituent Structure in German. Hans Uszkoreit. Lecture Notes No. 8.

Prolog and Natural-Language Analysis. Fernando C.N. Pereira and Stuart M. Shieber. Lecture Notes No. 10.

Working Papers in Grammatical Theory and Discourse: Interactions of Morphology, Syntax, and Discourse. M. Iida, S. Wechsler, and D. Zec (eds.), with an Introduction by Joan Bresnan. Lecture Notes No. 11.

Natural Language Processing in the 1980s: A Bibliography Gerald Gazdar, Alex Franz, Karen Osborne, and Roger Evans. Lecture Notes No. 12.

Information-Based Syntax and Semantics: Volume 1 Fundamentals. Carl Pollard and Ivan Sag. Lecture Notes No. 13.